DISCOVERING
THE WORK

How a stroke allowed me to discover a more symbiotic way of working with horses

Kathleen Lindley Beckham

Book Design by HMDpublishing

Cover photos by Montana Canter Photography

Contents

Introduction...4

Coloring Outside the Lines 9

It's Your Journey: Do Your Own Work 15

Be With Me 18

Lost Words 23

Thinking About Talking 28

Finding the Profound in the Mundane...............................32

Haltering 37

Bridling 41

It Depends....................................45

If We Quit, We Can't Help...................................49

On "Natural Horsemanship" 53

On Starting at the Beginning Rather Than at the End...............................56

The Long Walk 60

On Being a Good Student...................................64

Deliberate Practice 67

The Hearst Castle and Horsemanship 71

A Profound Quandary 76

Doing Our Time....................................80

Half-Broke Horses 84

The 1%: Managing the Corners 89

What I Learned From ChiChi 93

If It Walks Like a Duck and Quacks Like a Duck... 96

Thoughts on Teaching and Learning Feel 100

Wherever You Go, There You Are 104

What is "Broke"? 109

On Judging Progress 113

Filling In.....................................117

How I Almost Quit 122

Introduction

In the fall of 1994, I was 28 years old and a successful rider and trainer of jumping horses in southeastern Wisconsin. There was really nothing else I'd ever wanted to do aside from riding horses. When I'd graduated high school in 1984, I'd had no trouble obtaining a position teaching, riding, and showing at a hunter/ jumper barn. I was tall, willowy, and very strong from years in the saddle. I loved the horses, I loved showing, and I loved being successful in the horse business. The essay I'd written as a 13-year-old — "I am Going to be a Horse Trainer" — was coming to fruition.

That year, 1994, I had finally taken some time out of my busy schedule to visit some relatives in Aspen, Colorado, where I'd met their outdoorsy neighbor. I came home from Aspen with a long-distance relationship to add to my busy and fulfilling life. That fall, he came to visit me in Wisconsin, and we spent some time hiking the Kettle Moraine together, enjoying the beautiful fall foliage.

While on that hike, a wave of dizziness suddenly washed over me. "Whew!" I said, "I think I need to sit down for a second!"

I sat down, and I didn't get back up. Right after I sat down, my left side went limp, and I tipped over. I was mystified. My left arm and left leg wouldn't work. I couldn't get up. "This is so weird!" I thought. "This is what it must be like when an old person has a stroke."

At 28 years old, with no family history and no risk factors, I'd had a stroke. A blood clot had lodged in the right internal capsule of my brain and effectively knocked out all the motor skills on my left side. I couldn't stand or walk on my own.

At the emergency room, I insisted over and over again that no, I was not taking cocaine (one of the causes of "young strokes" it turns out). I was HIKING. I was not on "the pill" (another cause of "young strokes" in women). Heck, I didn't even eat red meat at the time. I was admitted to the hospital as the youngest resident of their stroke wing.

I was truly fortunate, because my stroke did not affect my speech or the cognitive areas of my brain. It simply knocked out every motor skill on my left side. Half of my tongue was paralyzed, half of my lips were paralyzed, and then my left arm and left leg didn't work at all. I had sensation; if you pricked me with a pin, I could feel it, but I couldn't snatch my hand away.

Days later, one of my physicians wrote in a report, "I have also initiated social service evaluation for potential funding sources for ongoing care, including disability and Title 19 benefits, if necessary, as the patient has significant neurologic involvement and will likely have some degree of long-term disability."

Being helpless and in the hospital is very humbling. If you're like me, and not accustomed to asking for help, it's a steep learning curve, and it's not like you have a choice. If I wanted to turn over in bed, I had to call a nurse. If I had to go to the bathroom, I had to call a nurse. If I wanted a friend to bring a specific food for me, I had to ask.

I slept a lot. I think this was partly my body healing — and using a massive amount of energy to do that — and partly avoidance. Nobody wakes up in the morning thinking they're going to become a 28-year-old stroke survivor. I slept parked in the hallway, sitting in a wheelchair. I slept through tests and procedures. I nodded off while doctors were talking to me. I couldn't help it.

I was in the hospital for two weeks, and during that time, we hit physical and occupational therapy pretty hard. Since my insurance had run out about a week into my stay, the hospital was anxious to discharge me as soon as was reasonable. When I left the hospital, I was walking carefully with a cane, and I basically had no practical use of my left hand. When a friend dropped me off at my apartment building, I realized that I could not get in the front door because I had to put an old key in a keyhole and turn it with one hand while turning a door knob with the other. I couldn't get into my own apartment. I sat in the entryway and cried until a kind neighbor passed through and let me in.

I couldn't open a milk carton. I couldn't button jeans or a shirt. I couldn't hook a bra. Pulling on socks one-handed was an Olympic-level athletic feat. I spent hours working on my left hand, carefully picking up a pill bottle off the coffee table, placing it deliberately on the floor, releasing it, and then picking it up again and putting it back on the coffee table, over and over, for hours. It took an extraordinary amount of thought and energy. I quit my job and dropped out of college.

I called up a good friend who had school horses and asked if she would let me ride one of her quiet ones. I just kind of needed to know that I still could, somehow. A couple days later, there I was, at my friend's barn after hours to ensure some privacy, realizing that it's hard to tack up a horse with one hand and that your balance is crap when half of your body is basically unable to support itself in space. It was hard. It was neither inspiring experience nor discouraging; it was more of a "this is just where we are right now" kind of experience. There was just a lot we didn't know.

A few weeks after I got out of the hospital, I did something that they teach you in therapy not to do: I stepped down off a curb with my left ("bad") foot and severely sprained my ankle. This is something I would do two more times (except those times, I'd do it while riding), and it would eventually cause me to have my left ankle surgically reconstructed.

I didn't have any family in Wisconsin, and although I had an excellent network of friends, they had their own lives to lead, and it was hard for them to help me out as much as they wanted to. Since I'd quit my job and dropped out of school, I decided it was a good time to relocate to Colorado, where my aunt and uncle could put me up and help me out. Aspen had a great public transportation system and excellent therapists and rehab facilities. I made the move and promptly bought a horse.

Now, as they say, hindsight is 20/20, and that may not have been the wisest thing for me to do right then, but that's what I did. I bought a five-year-old, grey Thoroughbred gelding, the kind of horse I felt accustomed to, and named him Ashcroft, after a ghost town near Aspen.

I was getting around okay at that point. I walked with a limp, my left arm didn't swing when I walked, and I didn't have a very good sense of where the left side of my body was in space, but I was pretty "functional." I realized that when people saw my limp, they assumed it hurt, so I learned to assuage their concerns by saying things like, "Oh, yes, I limp, but don't worry, it isn't painful. It just doesn't work that well."

I started riding Ashcroft, and it didn't take long for it to become a bit of a mess. Obviously, I wasn't riding with the body that I used to ride with, but that didn't stop me from trying to ride the way I used to ride. After all, that was all I knew. The way I rode at the time was kind of about "winning" and "not letting the horse get away with anything." It was, frankly, pretty adversarial and very physical. And I couldn't do it anymore. I just wasn't physically strong enough or coordinated enough. Furthermore, Ashcroft was not "playing along" at all, so we spent quite a bit of time getting absolutely nowhere — and worse yet, not liking each other much at all.

Thanks to what was most likely divine providence, I'd actually landed in a geographical hotbed for horsemanship clinics at the time. Everyone who was anyone in horsemanship lived in, worked in, or passed through Colorado around that time, so it was easy to start going to watch clinics on the weekends.

This was a world that, as much as I knew about horses, I didn't know anything at all about. This was about working with the horse's mind, about connecting with him and helping him agree with what we were doing. I had never even thought about those things before. Though I'd been a successful equestrian professional for years, I don't think I knew anything about how horses learn or different approaches to teaching horses. In my horse life, I'd mostly ridden horses that had already been trained by someone else before they got to me. I guess I was more of a "pilot" than anything else. So, when I ended up with a fairly "untrained" horse and I had new physical challenges, I didn't really know what I was doing. And Ashcroft was more than happy to let me know that.

It became increasingly clear to me that I was going to have to learn a way of working with horses that was, you could say, more "mental" and less "physical," one based on achieving peace rather than waging war, because that was going to be my only way forward. It wasn't so much an ethical choice for me at that point; it was supremely practical. To keep going, to carry on with horses, I was going to have to basically start over. The funny thing was that it didn't feel scary, or frustrating, or negative. It felt like a gift, an opportunity, a do-over. There were a lot of things in my life just then that I didn't have a whole lot of choice about, so it made sense to see the good in it and get on with it.

What I discovered, in my do-over, was that the horse is this beautiful, strong, explosive, amazing, kind, generous, peace-loving creature. I discovered that the horse is a magical creature, but he's also a gritty, honest, and brutal part of the natural world. Life with horses is soul-shattering.

I discovered that at the bottom of me is a willingness to plod, if necessary, on and on, forward. I discovered that I could consider quitting and then start again, over and over, daily if necessary. I discovered my "why."

And, best of all, I fell in love with The Horse all over again.

The following chapters tell my stories of discovery and transition as I have connected to horses in a deeper and more symbiotic way ever since.

Chapter 1

Coloring Outside the Lines

It is perhaps the horse's greatest contradiction: that an animal so big and so powerful can, simultaneously, be so very subtle. They can bite and kick each other powerfully and, then, in the next moment, dial that down to a glance or the flick of an ear.

Working with horses is not only a science; it's also an art in a lot of ways. It's about creativity and feel and making it up as we go along. Working with horses is a lot like the horses themselves: subtle and not-so-subtle all at the same time. The not-so-subtle stuff, I suppose, we could say is technique. That's the "press on this, and the horse will do that" kind of stuff. The subtle stuff is more along the lines of thoughts, attitudes, and "energy." I guess we could see the subtle and not-so-subtle stuff as layers of the same things. Some of the layers are thinner than others, and some are maybe so thin we can't even really see them.

The "energy" thing I mentioned is something that can be particularly daunting for some of us. Electricity is energy, and even if we can't see it, we accept that it exists (think: electric fence). We accept that the energy between two magnets exists despite its invisibility because we've all seen magnets move each other. Wind is energy; water is energy. We can extend this experience of energy's invisible power to say that thoughts, emotions, and attitudes are also energy. If technique is a thick layer in horsemanship, the thoughts, emotions, and attitudes that underlie our horsemanship are a thinner layer.

Language

Many of us haven't given much thought to the words we use in relationship to our horse work, but sports psychologists and coaches and motivational speakers have long acknowledged how powerful self-talk is. In other words, the words we use say a lot about the attitudes and beliefs that lie beneath that choice of words.

Years ago, it wasn't uncommon for me to describe a horse I was working with as "lazy," "looking to take advantage" of us, "trying to get out of work," or even "piggy." Now, if I'd used those same words to describe a person, I think we'd all agree that it would sound like I was describing someone who wasn't very nice, and it would also sound like I wasn't having very much fun. I thought I loved horses back then, but from the words I used to describe them, it sure didn't sound like it.

What if that "lazy" horse was stiff, sore, or confused? What if that horse who was "looking to take advantage" of me was just trying different things in an honest attempt to learn? What if what the horse was doing had nothing to do with me (perish the thought!)? We horse people kind of have this habit of criticizing our horse's character rather than describing a behavior neutrally (and really believing that they're not intentionally annoying us).

I used to have my clinic participants fill out a "clinic questionnaire" before they arrived, and one of the prompts was, "Describe your horse to me." Another question I asked was, "What are some things your horse does that you'd prefer he did differently?" What was interesting about this questionnaire was the number of horse owners who said, "Pushy" under "Describe your horse to me," but didn't mention it under, "What are some things your horse does that you'd prefer he did differently?"

What that told me is that these particular people were more likely to see "pushy" as a personality trait rather than a training problem. That gave me a lot to think about.

I worked with a dog trainer once who stressed that we needed to tell our dogs what *to* do, rather than what *not* to do. She claimed that telling a dog what *not* to do would leave a "void" or blank space that the dog would fill with *something*. As she saw it, the dog had to do something at any given time, so he might as well do something we prescribe to him. So, "Don't bark" becomes, "Come, sit, heel."

This idea is old news in sports psychology and coaching. Many coaches would confirm that they believe there's a big difference between a team that is playing to *win* and one that is playing to *not lose*. The difference is in the words and the energy and attitude carried by those words. Are we riding to have fun and connect with our horses (the positive goal), or are we riding to not get hurt or be scared (the negative goal)?

When we call a horse a name ("lazy," "piggy," "counterfeit"), we prevent ourselves from asking *why* the horse is doing what he's doing or isn't doing what he isn't doing by blaming it on his poor character. Thus, a few years ago, I made a conscious choice to believe that when a horse wasn't doing what I needed him to do, he either couldn't (physically or mentally) or didn't understand what I was asking him to do. I figured that whether it was true or not, this belief would give me somewhere to go and would keep the lines of communication open between me and the horse.

If we can modify our language to cast a more positive light on our horses, ourselves, and what is going on between us, what is possible? At the very least, what does it hurt? If I believe my horse is trying, I can believe I am trying. That's all any of us can do.

The Basics

It's funny, but the more I learn about horses, the more I feel like it's all about the basics. By the basics, I mean the B-A-S-I-C-S. For me, the basics are: go forward, turn left, turn right, stop, and back up. Everything a horse will be asked to do for the rest of his life (including spins, piaffes, pirouettes, opening gates, roping, etc.) will be a version of those five things. Everything.

I have a very good friend who is a multiple-degree black belt in Karate. She's been studying and practicing for many, many years. On the phone one night, as she explained that she was struggling to teach a large class filled with people of varying ages and abilities, she decided that her source of confidence in her Karate teaching was that, as she put it, "I know the basics." That really made an impression on me, particularly coming from someone with her skill and experience.

The thing about the basics is that if something is lacking at the most basic level of the basics, then we're building on sand, so to speak, rather than on rock. We're trying to put up the second floor of our building when we haven't finished framing the first.

There are a lot of reasons we can neglect the basics. There's time and money, of course. We just don't have time with a sale horse to do the basics. We don't have the money to do the basics because who wants to pay for a lesson to learn how to *stop*?? And it gets more complex from there. We can neglect the basics because our horse is particularly quiet or particularly smart, particularly cute or particularly well-bred. The thing is, the cute card kind of runs out when the cute horse doesn't understand how to stop and runs away with us.

We can also neglect the basics because we think we're "past" the basics, that those things don't apply to us. We can get to thinking that we can ride well enough to ride past the basics, through anything the horse may offer. Or, maybe we think we don't know *enough* to adhere to a good understanding of the basics. But, we have to start somewhere, and there's no time like the present.

The basics start on the ground, where it would be nice if our horse could go forward, turn left, turn right, stop, and back up with a minimum of pressure or trouble.

Of course, this raises the question of what, exactly, a "minimum of pressure" is. This is, of course, relative to the person making the judgment, but one way to look at it is to put the pressure that we use on a scale of 0 to 10, with 0 being no pressure and 10 being as much pressure as we can possibly use. For the most part, I try to get things to where I can use a 1 or less on that scale and get a consistent response. We may not start there, but that's what we're working toward. I'd call that a "minimum of pressure."

If we can do those basics with a minimum of pressure on the ground, then we need to get those same basics working under saddle. Again, it would be nice if our horse could go forward, turn left, turn right, stop, and back up consistently and with a minimum of pressure.

Time spent on the basics comes back to us exponentially down the line. Once we get the basics working consistently, when we move on, those transitions to the new stuff can be smoother and quicker. Also, and importantly, every riding horse needs to have a good understanding of the basics in order to be safe and useful.

Peace and Quiet

This is something that we don't really talk about much in relation to training horses, but I'm starting to think that it's a lot easier for a horse to learn something if they are quiet in their mind. And I'm not talking about external peace and quiet here; it's more of an internal peace and quiet. If the horse's mind is racing, troubled, or overwhelmed, he just can't take in new information.

Now, I'm not saying that a horse will never be bothered when we're working with him. That's going to happen sometimes, and sometimes it needs to happen so that the horse can get to a better place physically and mentally.

This might be one of those things that good horsemen do that we don't know they do because we don't really see them do it. If you closely watch folks who are really good with horses, you'll notice that they spend some time getting that horse quieted down and thinking and asking questions before they present the horse with new information; then, like magic, the information goes in, and the horse learns it.

It's the same with people. If our minds are full-up with miscellany or our thoughts are running off with us, it's difficult for us to be present and take in information. That miscellany can be anything from planning our grocery list to reviewing what we read in the latest issue of *Practical Horseman*. The kinds of thoughts that tend to run off with us are "what if's," fear, and self-doubt. Those thoughts can take up so much room that there's no room for much else.

If we can get to a place where our mind is quieter, we can see what our horse is offering for what it is. All that stuff that's cluttering up our minds will still be there when we get done working with our horse, and we can get back to it then.

I picked up a little magnet this summer at a book store that kind of summed up this idea for me:

Peace.
It does not mean to be in a place
where there is no noise, trouble
or hard work. It means to be in
the midst of those things and still
be calm in your heart.
(unknown)

That would be a nice place to be able to be *with* my horse, I think.

Chapter 2

••

It's Your Journey: Do Your Own Work

Many of us like to think of our horse work and horsemanship as a "journey," a path — sometimes straight, sometimes convoluted — that we all walk. Each of us walks an entirely unique path, determined by who we are, our history, and our circumstances. No two of us will walk exactly the same path. We might walk a similar or parallel path to someone else and have a traveling partner for a short or a long time, but in the end, our path is our own. We are responsible for it, and it's important that we realize that we are a volunteer (not a victim) on our path.

Most of us are studying horsemanship because we want to better our work (and, therefore, our life) in some way. In the beginning, the way we learn is usually through imitation. A teacher shows us something, and we imitate it to the best of our ability. We may have very little true understanding of what we're doing or why. We don't really "own" the information or the movements yet, but we go through the motions, and we think about the theories. At some point, hopefully, we start to "own" the movements and the knowledge, and we begin to understand both at a deeper level. We begin to be able to creatively combine movements and concepts, to problem solve, and to do the work with "feel" and mindfulness rather than simple mechanical imitation. This process takes time and practice.

This is true of many pursuits, not just horsemanship. Think of learning to dance with a partner. At first, a teacher shows us how to stand and how to move; then, they teach us some steps. We imitate the instructor and practice the movements and probably feel pretty clumsy and mechanical for a while. But, then, a transition starts to take place, and we begin to understand the steps and the movements and the why of all it, and something starts to flow. That's when dancing starts to feel good, and we start to feel some competence. At this point, we can start to improvise a bit and move away from pure imitation and toward ownership of our dancing.

It's the same with our horsemanship. There's a transition that happens, when we move from imitation to ownership. That's when we start doing our own work instead of doing an imitation of someone else's. That's when the work becomes a part of who we are.

The important thing to know here is that we really can *only* do our own work. We cannot do anyone else's work, nor can they do ours. Only Ray Hunt could do Ray Hunt's work, only Nuno Olivera could do Nuno Olivera's work, and that goes for every other master and every other teacher. Only you can do your own work.

If you are a beginner or an intermediate horseman, you may still be in a place of imitation, learning the work. Do this with gusto and awareness! Maximize your imitation experience, and practice well. This is a great and necessary stage of learning that we all revisit time and time again over our lifetimes, because as we gain mastery of a certain concept or movement, we become a beginner again at another.

Advanced horsemen on the road toward mastery can strive to walk our own path and to do our own work. We do not need to see what we do as imitation if it is part of who we are. We can own it and nurture it and take responsibility for it. We can walk our own path and let others walk theirs. If we choose, our horsemanship will become less about who we've imitated and more about who we are within and because of our work.

I want to add a special note here for female practitioners of the art of horsemanship. We often feel like we need to quote our male teachers and mentors to gain credibility and respect. This, too, is okay, for a time. Then, it becomes a crutch. We can be aware of when we do this, and we can hear ourselves as others hear us. When we can do that, we can start to transition to our own voice, and we can refer to our own experiences and knowledge and our own journey with the horses. At some point, we too have moved past the imitation of our teacher to doing our own work. That owning is both scary and liberating.

We can be happy about where we are on our path without being quite satisfied. After all, paths are made for movement.

Chapter 3

··

Be With Me

Some time ago, I spent my summers traveling the country to te-ach clinics and lessons and my winters living at a friend's farm in South Carolina. It never failed that I'd have the opportunity to pick up some horses during my travels and spend the winter in South Carolina "studying" them (working with them). They were all kinds of horses, and they were available to me for lots of different reasons, but many of them needed new addresses because they were not working out in their current ones.

It can be really fun and interesting to untangle these kinds of horses and help them feel better about things. Some of them became "keepers," while others became suitable for new homes, but what it did for me was give me the opportunity to get to know new horses, over and over, and spend six months to a year with them. This was very different than my day job, which was spending a few days with lots of different horses at clinics.

In some cases, I was unravelling their trouble, and in other cases, I was just a waypoint to another job assignment, but I learned lots from them either way. One winter, I bought one and was given one, and they got me thinking about what it means for a horse to "be with me."

Arlo, the horse I bought, is the control group for this discussion. He was a five- or six-year-old, off-the-track Thoroughbred. He had no run in him, and he was a big, heavy horse. He was sort of an example of how random breeding can be, because he exhibited few to none of the characteristics of a good racehorse. Arlo came off the track (having never raced) and went to a horseman who played with him, made friends with him, and let him enjoy being around people. Then, he came to the farm in South Carolina, where he sat in the pasture and did ground work with one of my friends for another year. About the time he was ready to ride, I bought him.

The thing about Arlo was that, as far as I could tell, his mind was still in its fairly "original state." He was simple, confident, curious, completely and utterly open-minded, and loved people. Now, this was partly because of his unique character, but partly because of how he'd been brought on. Arlo kind of became my "control group," as I thought about this stuff because when I put information into Arlo, it came out just how I put it in. That made him pretty easy. I didn't have to beg Arlo to do anything. He just didn't seem to see any reason not to try to do just about anything.

When Arlo was with people, he was fully engaged. He was open and honest and curious. He was interactive without being obnoxious, and if you didn't need him, he went to sleep, literally. If he didn't understand something, he just said so, and there was no drama. It was okay for him to not know how to do something.

It was good to have Arlo to compare these other horses to, because I could start to see how far these other horses had come from what had perhaps been their original selves. I wasn't there, but, dang, only PEOPLE could have made some of these horses THAT complicated! I don't know when these horses became the way they were, but my guess is that it could have gone as far back as the way they were started or the way they were halter broke. Maybe not, but it sure could have.

Then there was Toby. Toby was a 12-year-old unregistered Thoroughbred who was bred to be a show horse. Other people had ridden and jumped him. I had a little trouble catching Toby at first, and when I stuck to it and hung in there, I noticed that, here and there, Toby tended to lay his ears back and look grumpy. I think he was expecting me to quit on him, and I think he was kind of frustrated when I didn't. By being hard to catch, I guess you could say that, given his druthers, Toby was "opting out" of the relationship and the things we might do together before we even began.

With more work, what I started to see was that Toby had trouble being with people. If he was with a person, he felt like he had to push on them or position them in some way. If he couldn't push on them, he opted to leave (bolt). There wasn't a whole lot in between. He couldn't just "be" with a person and feel good about it. This was a pretty awkward place for Toby. He was in a kind of twilight between a world WITH people, which he didn't understand, and a world WITHOUT people, which was impractical. He was stuck, and he knew it. He shook, sucked his tongue, and got diarrhea when he was confused. He was either defensive and trying to push people away, or he was actively leaving. He was just doing the only things he knew how to do. My job was to show him all the gray areas in between...and, boy, was it hard work for both of us.

Then there was Polly. Polly was an adorable little grade mare that I picked up on the road, and she kind of had something totally different from Toby going on. People coming around her actually seemed to "excite" her. I could see that some folks might see what she did as "affection," but if you've been around horses a lot, you'd notice that what Polly did felt...well, just weird.

For instance, Polly was easy to catch and halter, but once we reached the hitch rail by the tack room, it was clear that she'd become "elevated" mentally. Her head would go up, and she'd become obviously restless. If you walked away from her, she would quiet, but when you walked back to her, she'd become busy again. I had her on the high tie one day, and I watched her watching me. If she knew I was watching her, she pawed and paced. If she couldn't see me watching her, she was quiet and just stood there with a hip cocked. If I approached her, she would whinny. If I walked away, she would quiet.

What I realized was that Polly's "be with humans" felt kind of frantic, like being around people made her mind race in some weird, anxious, but not scared way. It had a very odd feel to it, and it was kind of a tangled mess.

How a horse feels when he's with us is important. Most of the time, it's probably more important to him than it is to us. That's because he sees it more honestly than we do. Maybe we think he feels good about being with us because we give him food. But it might be the food he feels good about, not us. How does he feel about us without the food? That would be the kicker, wouldn't it? How do horses want to feel when they're with us? They want to feel like a horse. They want to feel comfortable and confident and quiet. Horses who are good friends seem to spend a lot of time just standing, being together quietly, in companionship, not in the throes of some deep emotional passion. Very passionate relationships are mostly discouraged in the horse world because they cause stress and instability in the herd.

So, how can we tell how our horse feels when we come around? Well, an easy project to work on is to watch his eyes and ears and general posture. When we approach a horse, we'd really like him to kind of "reach" for us — mentally, emotionally, and physically. A reach and a push are two different things. Think of the difference in people; the same holds true here. We'd like the horse to look at us as we approach and put an ear on us. We'd like him to continue to keep an eye connected to us as we work around him or halter him. Does he lean away from us or flinch when we touch him? Is his skin hard and tight, or soft and elastic? Many horses who are a bit bothered by people will look away; they'll look away when we pet them or when we present the halter. That looking away is a mental leaving. That horse just left mentally. He'd leave physically if he could. What does it take to get him back? Can I tap my leg and bring him back? Scuff my boot in the dirt? Touch him on the neck? Reach out to him mentally?

The next question is, how can I get him to want to be with me and stay with me? I approached this question in a philosophical way a few years back and decided what I'd do is "become the person my horse needs me to be." I'm assuming this will be a lifelong project. We can teach a horse that he HAS to be with us, that he doesn't have a choice. We can teach him to look at us and keep track of us, or else. But there's another layer in there, where the horse truly WANTS to be with us, and it feels good to both of us to be together. One of the hardest things for a horse person to do is to honestly see how a horse feels when he's with us. However, we don't want to delude ourselves about this. Sometimes looking at this honestly is going to hurt. I'm still working on it, and I don't always get it completely right. But I try to stand back and honestly assess how things are between me and the horse I'm working with. I'd like him to change a little and me to change a little, and through those changes, we find a balance and harmony (lack of friction) between us.

Not long ago, I was re-reading Ray Hunt's Think Harmony with Horses, and a sentence in the second paragraph of the first page of the introduction fairly LEAPT off the page, as if I'd never seen it before. As many times as I've read that book, that sentence had never registered. The sentence reads, "Mentally, your horse should not weigh anything." I'll be chewing on that for a long time, a lifetime, really. What would it be like for our horse to "mentally... not weigh anything"? That's something for each of us to figure out for ourselves.

Chapter 4

···

Lost Words

My friend Sara has said that I am "ruled by words" and she is not. She makes up words sometimes, and it makes me a little crazy. I've always been fascinated by words. I even remember my mother reading the *Reader's Digest* feature "It Pays to Enrich Your Word Power" to me every month when I was a kid. Words are how we communicate, and the words we choose to use say something about us. Or not.

A long time ago, I subscribed to what was then called *The Trail Less Traveled* magazine, and I was also a member of one of the very first internet-based horsemanship discussion groups. Even then I was sensitive to the words that horsemanship aficionados used. They were new to me at the time, and I remember thinking about them and rolling them over my tongue and around my mind. It reminded me of when I was a barn rat as a kid and sat around the barn, listening and watching. If I heard grown-ups mention a horse with a "splint," then I'd go look at the horse and see what a splint was. I learned a whole language that way as a kid. As an adult, I learned multiple "horse languages," and one of them was related to horsemanship.

As I've studied the language of horsemanship over the years, I've noticed that we just no longer hear some of the words that were once common parlance for students of horsemanship — at least at the time of this writing.

One of the phrases we used to hear often in horsemanship was "filling in," which is, quite simply, when the horse does something correctly even though we've asked incorrectly. Filling in is an act of charity on the part of the horse. It used to be that filling in was seen as something positive that a horseman could get his or her horse prepared to do at some point. It was seen to represent a positive relationship between a horse and a person.

However, I don't know when I last heard someone talk about filling in or something like it. Well, actually, I did hear actor Matt Damon talk about it a while ago, but he didn't call it that. In a *Today Show* interview about shooting the movie *True Grit*, he said that if he rode his horse up and missed his mark by a bit, the horse would lean over a little to get him where he needed to be for the camera. Damon seemed to think this was pretty cool and a mark of how beautifully trained the movie horses were.

These days, it's not uncommon to hear long lists about why our horses WON'T do things. "My horse will only get in the trailer if it's a step-up," "I'm sure I wasn't focused, and that's why my horse didn't canter," "The dog was running around, so my horse couldn't tie quietly."

Now, don't get me wrong; there is truth in all of these statements. I wish all of us could do everything we do with our horses perfectly all the time, but quite often something is not going to be right, and I think it's realistic to hope that our horses could fill in sometimes and do it for us anyway. Don't good friends and partners (and employees) do that? Maybe when the horse fills in, he's rewarding OUR try, just as we strive to reward his. It's a matter of balance and mindfulness.

If we didn't have horses who could fill in, we would have no kids' horses, school horses, or handicapped rider assistance horses, and many of us would have never learned how to ride, or we'd have gotten killed or hurt in the process. Part of learning to ride used to be graduating from horses who filled in A LOT to horses who filled in less and, perhaps eventually, to horses who didn't fill in at all. This used to be the way "learning to ride" was structured. Today, it's not uncommon to see a beginner rider with a horse who can't fill in and to see everyone (including those around them) suffering as a result.

There's a practical side to a horse being able to fill in. Say you live in an area that has the possibility of natural disasters, like forest or wild fires. You may get an evacuation notice and have to shove three horses, four dogs, two unhappy cats, your family, and your most prized irreplaceable personal possessions into your trailer and pickup truck in the space of an hour, as sparks and ash fall, fire sirens sound, and your cell phone rings off the hook. If your horse can't fill in a bit for you there, you might not get out.

It is an honorable quest to strive to get as good as we can at this stuff, and I'm not saying that we shouldn't get as good as we can so that our horse doesn't have to fill in, but it's all about balance. Sometimes we fill in for him, and sometimes he fills in for us. Maybe a reasonable place to start is to just be mindful of when and if our horse is filling in for us and be thankful for it when it happens. That feels like a partnership to me.

Another term we don't hear much anymore is a mouthful: anthropomorphizing. This is, in short, the act of attributing human characteristics to something that is not human. Now, as humans, I don't think we really have any other way to see the world than from our own perspective and frame of reference, so this is likely a very natural thing for us to do. We won't go into the philosophical revolving door on that one. Let's just look at the horsemanship part of it.

For example, a student was using one of my horses for a lesson, and she had a bit of trouble catching this horse — not a lot, just a little. I hadn't told the student that this horse did tend to leave when someone tried to catch her because I didn't want to set up that expectation for the student, but this particular horse would walk off when any of us went to get her. I thought it felt a bit like she'd been chased off in the past and she was just kind of looking for that to happen. She'd leave and then get caught. She got caught 100% of the time, but she just left first.

I asked my student how catching went, and she said, "Well, I don't think she feels like working today."

That's why a HUMAN would avoid being caught right away, but I knew for a fact that this horse would work all day, and I hadn't ever found the bottom of her. This example shows how we run the risk, when we anthropomorphize, of attributing negative character traits to horses who are just doing things that, in their own minds, may have a perfectly good reason or a neutral value. Or, it could just be instinct, and that's all.

Anthropomorphizing can cause us to not be able to see things the horse does at face value or from his point of view. Because of who horses are (prey animals, herd animals, etc.), certain things are important to them that aren't important to us, and vice versa. When we project human characteristics and values inaccurately onto a horse, we can create difficulties in communication, as well as stress and dysfunction. The amount of time it takes to construct anthropomorphic thoughts can throw our timing off or take us out of the moment and out of the arena mentally.

It's human to interpret a nicker or whinny as affection. Maybe it is "affection"; maybe it isn't. People sometimes interpret pushy horses as affectionate. Sometimes we're right on, and sometimes it doesn't do any of us any good. Again, it's about balance and mindfulness. Sometimes that horse is simply doing something that has benefitted him in the past, and it doesn't actually have anything to do with us or with him experiencing human-like emotions.

Anthropomorphizing can range from attributing motives to a horse's behavior in the moment to constructing elaborate fictional stories about a horse's past. These stories can be crippling to a horse's learning, and, worse yet, if someone along the horse's path mistakes this fiction as truth, the horse may have to live with that story for the rest of his life.

I think a lot of anthropomorphizing happens because we need ways to describe what's happening with our horse, which is totally understandable. For instance, we might say, "My horse is giving me the middle finger like a teenager!", when what's really happening is that our horse has just done something (which may or may not have anything to do with us) that makes us FEEL the same as when a teenager flips us "the bird." See the difference there? We are responsible for our feelings. Our feelings don't necessarily accurately define what our horse did. We may say, "He is doing that to scare me," because what the horse is doing is scaring us. That doesn't mean that he's deliberately doing that to scare us. He could be doing whatever it is for completely different reasons.

Current science shows that horses are only capable of the simplest of emotions. The same science also suggests that horses are only capable of a certain amount of rational planning and thought. If we forget this and anthropomorphize in the wrong way, or at the wrong time, it could be disastrous to our relationship and the training process. How we address our tendency to anthropomorphize is largely about our awareness of our own internal monologue.

As we go along our horsemanship journey, wherever we are in that journey, we can develop mindfulness regarding these topics and many others. For me, being mindful is about having an open mind. As I become mindful and aware, I do not always discover what I expect or what I already know. I do not always see what I think I'm going to see. Often, mindfulness leads to unexpected discoveries, new truths, and perhaps new beliefs. That's pretty exciting.

Chapter 5

··

Thinking About Talking

I've spent a lot of time in my life thinking about talking.

I like to try different things to see what happens. For a while, I practiced talking only when I was asked a question or had something of substance or purpose to contribute to the interaction, and I found that if I adhered to that standard, I often ended up speaking very little. This caused me to notice how much, in general, people talk. People talk A LOT. I'm not sure how much they actually have to say most of the time, but they sure talk A LOT, regardless.

As this relates to horsemanship, I think perhaps because we humans rely so much on verbal communication, it's hard for us to imagine a culture in which there's very little talking, like the equine culture. Sure, they talk a little audibly, but if we pay attention, a good deal of their verbal communication only comes out in stressful situations. Horses don't, as a rule, "talk" like the horse in the *War Horse* movie or the TV show *Yellowstone*. They don't nicker in complete sentences like that. Horses live in a largely silent world, and I think they long for peace and quiet.

If you're around horse people long enough, you may start to notice how often we put words in our horse's mouths. I am terribly guilty of this myself. I've started to wonder how much good this actually does for us or our horses. This is a big part of the anthropomorphic relationship we can have with our horses. If we anthropomorphize too much, we skew the relationship with the horse and things start to get dysfunctional. After all, a horse/human relationship is different than a human/human relationship. It seems to me that it's a bit of a constant exercise in awareness to keep the horse a horse in the relationship and to keep ourselves from trying to make it a person, since those are the kinds of relationships we're most familiar with...well, people and dogs. Lots of us are familiar with relationships with dogs, so we might think a horse/human relationship is similar to a dog/human relationship.

I got to thinking about all this, and I started thinking about my working horse. When I go to the field, he always acknowledges me. Most times, he will walk up and check in with me, even if I am there to get another horse. If we haven't done anything together in a while, he may take an opportunity to be rubbed on a bit and will just stand with me for a bit before moving off again to do his normal horsey business in the field. My "rule" is that I acknowledge any horse out there who acknowledges me, so the route to the horse I'm actually after can be a bit circuitous.

Some folks might see this kind of stuff as a horse showing "affection" toward me when I walk out there, but it doesn't feel like that, really. It might look like that to some people. Maybe that's how humans would show affection, hanging around and asking for touches. Sounds about right.

Then, other folks might say that's a bored or hard-working horse looking to come out and do something. "Me, me, pick me! I want to go do something!" might be the words those folks would put in my horse's mouth.

One day when I walked out there, I saw my horse turn and start to walk my way. Then he stopped and just stood there, looking at me. Ready. And it came to me. Another set of words to put in my horse's mouth were, "I am here."

"I am here." Period. End of sentence. Nothing else. No action. No emotion. Simple. That sounded more like something a horse might say.

How often do we say something that clear and meaningful to our horses? We talk in long convoluted paragraphs full of bunny trails, emotions, stories, and histories. When we ask our horses to do something, it's another paragraph. "Canter, please, please, please, but on the correct lead, and don't buck, and don't go too fast, and don't bounce me loose, and oh, I need to steer, and I hope I don't look a fool like that one time when I was cantering on the trail 10 years ago and my other horse skittered sideways and I kind of hung off the side for a few strides and all my friends laughed at me...who all was on that ride? I think there were five or six of us, and if I had been riding in the back, no one would have seen it, but since I was in front, they all saw it and laughed. So oh, yeah, don't do that...."

Another thing that humans do *all the time*? They answer a different question than was asked. I really got to study this when I was on the road. I asked people a LOT of questions, and I got to study their answers. People very often answer not the question that was asked, but a totally different question! Start listening for it, and you'll hear it everywhere! What if we do that with our horses? What if the question they ask is exactly the question they need an answer to, yet we answer a completely different question? What must that be like for them?

The horse just doesn't seem to work like that. His main motivations are to be physically safe and then to be as comfortable as possible. It's pretty simple to him, really. He is either comfortable or uncomfortable.

I think I'm going to spend some time practicing saying "I am here" when I am around my horses and in my life and see if I can just put a period on that sentence. If we're looking for a project to develop our awareness and improve our horsemanship, we could start to minimize our speech, even for just short periods at a time. We could pay attention to how many times we use the personal pronouns "I," "me," and "my" during the day. How much time do we spend talking about ourselves? How much time do we spend talking just to hear ourselves talk? Are we allergic to quiet? Do we have to fill every silence with chatter? Can we make our personal world quiet enough that there's room for the mostly silent horse?

We can pay attention to how silent our horse's world is. We can watch how clearly he communicates with other horses (if you can't watch your horse in a herd, watch others.). We can look for and find the periods on the ends of the sentences. We can appreciate the simplicity of their world.

∙∙∙

Chapter 6

Finding the Profound in the Mundane

Years ago, when my horse Daisy was a four-, coming five-year-old, we'd been having a lot of trouble with bridling. I'd started Daisy midway through her three-year-old year, and she'd bridled fine for almost a year, but she suddenly (it seemed to me) began literally running backwards from the bridle. When I did finally get her feet still, she would lean backward and lock her feet and jaw. From there, I'd get her bridled as quietly as I could, but it didn't feel very good to either of us.

The Buckaroos tend to move a young horse out of the snaffle bit and into the rawhide hackamore about the time their mouth turns into a mess of caps popping off and permanent teeth coming in. Thus, I decided that using a hackamore was a good idea for Daisy, and we successfully changed over to the hackamore for about 18 months. Of course, we didn't have any of the bridling issues with the hackamore that we'd had with the bridle.

Nevertheless, when Daisy's teeth had grown up and it was time to come back into the snaffle, I found we still had the bridling issue. She carried the bit fine now that her mouth was stable, but what had perhaps begun as a physical discomfort issue had become a behavioral training issue regarding the process of bridling itself. Thus, it was time to address it as such.

It's worth noting that I COULD bridle Daisy by myself. It didn't take half a football team to get it done or anything, but it didn't meet my standards. It didn't feel good between us, and it was certainly not something I'd show to a student and say, "This is a pretty ideal example of bridling."

I was kind of stuck with the whole thing. I'd used the techniques and ideas I was familiar with, and things had changed so far and no further. So, I swallowed my pride and asked my friend Jim to take a look at it with me and perhaps point out some things I was missing.

Jim watched me and Daisy do our thing for a bit. Then, he asked me to just tip her head toward me when I went to put the bridle on. When I did this, I could feel the rigidity of Daisy's whole spine, down to her feet. Holy cow! I'd been so focused on her head and jaw that I hadn't felt how HARD her whole body got when the bridle was presented. That explained why she leaned backward and locked her jaw. Her mind was leaving out the back door, and she was locking up her body because that was the best she could do to follow her mind. If I'd have let her body go with her mind, she'd have run away backward.

As Jim and I talked through what he was seeing and what I was feeling, I decided to back up to haltering and have Jim look at that too, and lo and behold, there it was again, but smaller: Daisy leaning backward, just a little, away from the halter!

In his book *Think Harmony with Horses*, Ray Hunt briefly talks about how when we "reach" for our horse, we'd like him to "reach" back for us. Ray used that word, "reach," and I really liked that word in the context in which he used it. I can reach for my horse mentally, emotionally, and/or physically. Then, my horse can reach back to me mentally, emotionally, and/or physically. Or not. When I go to the pasture, I reach for my horse mentally first, and she may flick an ear when she hears or sees or feels me. That's her reaching back to me. Then, when I approach with the halter, I reach for her physically, and it'd be nice if she reached for me physically then too. After all, a horse who's reaching isn't pushing.

So, that was kind of what I started to look for: when I reached for Daisy, what did she do? Did she reach for me? Was she in-different? Did she recoil? Did she escape? When I started paying attention, I realized that there were dozens of times each day that I "reached" for Daisy and was oblivious to what she did in response.

That was a good bit of what I was missing with Daisy and why bridling was so troublesome between us. There was no reach in her. I was reaching, but she was withdrawing. And it went all the way back to the halter. And with the halter, it went all the way back to the presentation of the halter. When I slowed the whole process down and paid attention (rather than haltering thought-lessly with no feel or awareness), I could feel the single moment when Daisy withdrew and we lost all "reach" between us. Once we moved to the bridle, the withdrawal grew exponentially.

I had my work cut out for me. I knew that in order to get the whole thing softer and feeling better all the way through, I nee-ded to get that reach working for us in everything we did. I nee-ded to be aware when Daisy withdrew and make sure that ended in a reach instead. She needed to get confident in that reach, and then it could get soft.

One of the things I need to acknowledge here is that I had TAUGHT Daisy to withdraw instead of reach. She had a lot of reach in her when I got her, and she had some push too. When I took the push out of her (doing the best I could at the time), I took the reach out too. I could write a whole book on how we worked on getting that reach back in there. I think how we did it is less important than the fact that we did it, period. We didn't use food, and I didn't really use any substantial degree of pres-sure. What I did was study how it felt to "draw" a horse in the round pen and then get that feel working during haltering and bridling. That's the best way I can describe it. It'd look different with different horses and different people, anyway, but if you're really interested knowing more about it, feel free to ask me if you see me sometime, and I can show you a couple of things.

This bridling stuff was a really big deal for me and Daisy. I can't speak so much for her as I can for myself, so I'll just focus on why it was so important for me. Once I began to examine the problem, I found that it went further back in our interactions than I thought it did. It turned out to be the embodiment of that seeming riddle, "What happened before what happened happened?" As usual, there was plenty that happened before what happened happened. In order to truly make things better, I had to go back to what happened before what happened happened and then move forward again from there. It was a lesson in humility, patience, and responsibility.

There are a bunch of reasons why I decided to tell this story. You'll get out of it what you get out of it, but let me offer a few takeaways that have really stuck with me so far.

1. Most of us are terrified of making "mistakes" with our horses or "screwing our horse up." We're doing the best we can at any one point in time. Two or three years from now, if we're working hard, we may have more technique, more mileage, more confidence, a better understanding, a different feel, etc. That will change how we go about things. If we keep a horse long enough, we'll end up living with work we did a few years ago. It's not a mistake; it's just where we are. So, we're always going to need to go back and change some things when we develop a different feel or explore some other ideas, if the horse is willing. In other words, it's not about mistakes; it's about developing an organic relationship with the horse, with ourselves, and with our individual journey.

2. The little stuff can be SO important. Sometimes students actually apologize to me for wanting to work on something as "simple" as leading or haltering or saddling their horse, but I think that this is the profound stuff, the stuff where having things to standard and everyone feeling good about it is so important. What I found was that me and Daisy were starting our time together with a huge disconnection between us,

and that's what I was trying to build each day's work on. I had to decide if that's what I wanted our life to be like. Sure, I COULD ride her, but how much better would she ride if she haltered and bridled better? We get good at what we practice. I was practicing a lack of awareness and feel and skipping things that weren't working well so that I could ride. That's not the kind of horseman I wanted to be.

3. Things can change, and it's not a matter of "fault." While I am responsible for what happened with Daisy and her bri-dling, it's not my "fault." The best way I can think of to ac-cept that responsibility in a positive way is to recognize, "If I was good enough to teach her THAT, I'm certainly good enough to teach her THIS." I had to get to a bit different place on my path in order to do it, but what's the rush? If we can accept where we are and do the work needed to move to another place, I don't know that we have a lot to complain about. So, I won't complain. I'm just glad I can get a bridle on my horse now and we both feel good about it.

4. Horsemanship (at least my own horsemanship) is a circle, or circle upon circle upon circle, or maybe a spiral. I think one of the first things an instructor taught me was how to halter and then bridle a horse. Now, here I am, decades later, work-ing on how to halter and then bridle a horse. These "simple" things don't go away; we don't learn them and leave them behind. As our awareness and our feel grows, so does the standard to which and the beauty with which we can perform such "mundane" tasks.

Chapter 7

Haltering

Like I noted earlier, horsemanship seems to be a bunch of concentric, interlocking, and overlapping circles and spheres, or maybe it's a spiral. Just when we think we've got something mastered, we get a hint that there's another layer of mastery out there to be had within that specific skill. At least that's how it seems to work for me. It's kind of like hiking in the mountains. You go up and up and up, and when you get to the top of the mountain you've hiked up, you can look out and see the tops of all the other mountains you could summit. From the bottom, you can only see the one you're hiking up, but from the top, you can see how immense the task is. Horsemanship is kind of like that.

I'm always working a lot on haltering and bridling my horses. These are tasks that are easy to do mechanically, without much feel or mindfulness, because we do them so often and they feel like such mundane tasks. To be honest, a lot of times I know I wasn't mindful about my haltering or bridling because my mind was already working on the "fun" stuff: RIDING!!!! So, I like to constantly remind myself to be mindful about haltering and bridling.

Winter can be a good time to start a project like this. We might have restricted time and daylight or poor footing, but we can halter our horse with quality regardless. If he halters well, there will be other things that are working well, because of the ways all the things in a horse tie together.

Haltering is important, because if we're mindful about it, we can get a lot of information about a horse from how he halters. Most horses will basically bridle how they halter, so if we work on haltering, we're also working on our bridling. Also, we've got an opportunity to take a leadership and relationship role with our horse right away by asking that they halter a certain way, with a certain feel.

Keep in mind that what follows is just one of an infinite number of ways to halter a horse. It's just a way I've been using that seems to help with a bunch of things that have become important to me with my horses. You can do this with any kind of halter, so that's not of critical importance for what I'm talking about here.

First, I ALWAYS have my halter and lead rope organized when I approach my horse. It's a bit rude to walk up to a horse and be all in a mess with one's halter and rope. It's kind of like showing up for a meeting with your fly undone and shirt buttons unbuttoned. We need to organize our halter and rope so we're able to move smoothly and straightforwardly when we get to our horse.

Once I reach my horse, I hold the crown piece of the halter in my left hand and kind of hug my horse around the neck, with my left arm under his neck and my right arm over the top of his neck. I feed the crown of the halter to my right hand, and I bring that toward me, over the top of the neck, and end up with the knot or buckle of the halter in my left hand. This forms a complete loop around my horse's neck and allows me to use the crown piece of the halter to direct my horse's head down and toward me. I'd like him to reach for the halter eventually, and this is the start. I'd also like him to halter at a comfortable height, say between my knees and my shoulders, so that I'm not on my tippy-toes as I halter him, as he leans back away from the halter. And, I'd like him balanced on all four feet and soft through his body and his mind.

When I use the halter to direct him toward me, I'm already thinking of the halter (or my hands on him) being connected not just to his head, but to his mind, body, and feet. This is a spot where we can practice feeling the WHOLE horse through that physical connection that we've just made with him, and we can feel the quality of his yield (or lack thereof). There's a difference between a horse who is reaching for me or the halter and a horse who is pushy. I'd like him to reach without pushing. I certainly don't want him to bump or bash me rudely with his head or drag me off.

With my horse's head tipped down and slightly toward me, with a soft arc (not a rigid arc) through his topline (vertically and laterally), I direct his nose into the halter. Interestingly, this is the same soft arc we might want to ride him in later. Then, I finish settling the halter into the proper position on his head, with awareness. I work to keep the horse connected to me during all of this, with his eyes and ears tilted toward me rather than away. A lot of times horses will start to hunt up the nose opening of the halter, so if my horse starts to do that, I'll certainly get myself set up so he can do that and we'll feel like it's really a team effort and I bring the thumbs for the buckles and knots. I finish buckling or tying my halter with my horse turned softly toward me, and off we go.

It's worth noting here that doing something mindfully doesn't necessarily mean doing it slowly or hesitantly. Sometimes, if we pause too much, the horse will get confused and fill that space with something. Thus, smooth, assured movement is the goal. Look and feel like you know what you're doing, and study what that feels like.

Unhaltering is important too because how we unhalter will set up how we will halter next time. Unhaltering looks and feels a lot like haltering. I ask my horse to reach out, down, and toward me with his head, and I slip the nose of the halter off his nose, returning to the position where I started, with the crown of the halter over the top of my horse's head/neck so that I can direct him into that soft arc through his spine, while his eyes and ears remain connected to me. Once he's connected and settled and soft, with his head down, breathing well, I drop the halter off him.

Every day, we have many opportunities to further our horsemanship skills. Studying mundane, everyday tasks and doing them mindfully and with conscious feel while also asking our horse to do these tasks to a high standard can provide benefits that reach far into our horsemanship. Our intentional interactions with our horse start not when we get on, but when we show up in his proximity. Depending on our set-up, our "interaction" with our horse may start when he recognizes the sound of our vehicle coming. From that moment, he is interacting with us. He's thinking about us even if we are unaware of his acknowledgement.

Chapter 8

· ·

Bridling

Bridling our horse is another one of those things that we do A LOT. It can be easy to just kind of mechanically shove the bridle on so that we can get in the saddle and ride because it's easy to get a bit thoughtless about things we do repetitively. But bridling, like haltering, is a great place to check in and connect with our horse every day, consciously building an increasingly beautiful and thoughtful ritual between us.

So, let's look at the how-to. Remember, there are an infinite number of ways to nicely and correctly bridle a horse, so what follows is not the only "right" way; it's just "a" way. I expect my own bridling will continue to evolve in the future. So, my advice is to just see if there might be something helpful in here for you and your horse. With a green horse, we might set aside a session or more to work on teaching bridling, but with a more solid grown-up horse, we might just set aside our normal bridling time to work on this. Eventually, the idea is to do this everyday task with mindfulness and respect rather than setting aside special time for it.

One of the prerequisites to bridling any horse (green or solid) is having a good, quiet, and soft head-down cue. Different people achieve this different ways, but the most common ways are with the halter and our hands. With a halter, I want to be able to take the bottom loop of my rope halter, where the lead rope attaches, apply soft pressure downward, and have the horse follow that feel so that I can put him wherever I need him. If I don't have a halter, I want to be able to do the same thing with my hands: one hand on his poll and one on the bridge of his nose. A horse can't be "too good" at letting us guide and position his head.

If our horse is worried or particularly confused about bridling (colts included), it can be helpful to leave a halter on and just practice bridling over the halter. We can then use that halter to position his head rather than getting busy with the bridle while the horse is already worried or confused. If I feel like there's any chance that I might have to chase that horse's head around during the bridling process, I leave that halter on him and bridle over it.

When we bridle, we need to decide what to do with our reins, particularly loop reins (like roping reins, English reins, or mecate reins). Some folks like to put the reins over the horse's head so that the horse doesn't end up completely loose, and other folks don't like the idea of putting the reins over the horse's head before he's completely bridled in case he leaves and takes the bridle with him. This, I'd say, is up to you, as it's your horse and your rig.

Whatever you decide to do with your reins, the next thing is positioning the horse's head for bridling and then presenting the bridle. I like to bring the horse's head to my "lap" for bridling. I tend to use the bridle itself to bring his head to me if he hasn't already done this. Eventually, I would like the horse to hunt the bridle, so every step of this process is designed to help him learn to do that. I take the crown of the bridle in my right hand and keep my left hand available for the bit and lower parts of the bridle. I run my right hand up and rest my right forearm between the horse's ears, adjusting the height of the bridle with that right hand. To position the horse's head, I put the headstall of the bridle about half-way over the horse's head, with the bit under his chin (in the curb-strap groove), the off-side cheek strap running across the off-side of his head, and the top of the crown in my right hand between his ears. With the bridle here, I can draw the horse's head to my lap.

Now, some folks, especially folks who have been taught how to bridle a horse in a mostly "English" riding environment, might have been taught to put their right arm UNDER the horse's jaw. The problem with this is that if the horse gives in to the pressure of the person's arm/shoulder under his head, it can teach the horse to raise his head during bridling. If I think about a short person, a child, or a frail person needing to bridle the horse, I'd rather he be thinking "down" than "up."

Right here is a cool place where we can feel for braces in the horse's body. If we're touching him, we should be able, at a level appropriate to our experience, to feel braces anywhere in his body, from his jaw and his poll to his spine and his feet. Any brace we feel in the horse's body is representative of a brace in his mind, so this can be a valuable place to assess our horse's physical and mental state.

Once the horse has his head down and bent slightly into us, we can present the bit. My goal is to have the horse open his own mouth for the bit. Lots of horses are accustomed to having their jaws pried open for the bit, so it can take a LONG time for some horses to get to where they'll take the bit on their own. I don't mind spending quite a bit of time on this spot over a horse's lifetime. If I knew a quicker way to accomplish this willingness, I'd do it, but this is what I've been working with at this point.

With the bridle positioned as above, we can drop the bit into our left hand, controlling the height with our right hand. Here, I'll take the bit and position the joint of the snaffle (or the middle of whatever bit we're using) directly where the horse's top and bottom teeth meet and make sure the skin of his lips and muzzle are out of the way. If I can avoid prying the horse's jaw open here, I certainly will. Sometimes I can just wait, and the horse will either take the bit or start to play with it. If that happens, I can release it and take the bit back to the chin groove to build that willingness to interact with the bit. I can also let the horse mouth the bit and experiment with chewing on it with his incisors. Lots of horses are afraid of the bit hitting their teeth, so if we can give them some time to touch the bit with their teeth, it can help them build confidence. If the bit gets set in the slot between the upper and lower teeth and the horse is really locked up and braced, I massage his gums or move his muzzle around softly to suggest that he soften up and think about unlocking his jaw. If a horse is really locked up, it can take a long time for him to willingly open his mouth and take the bit himself. With a really locked-up horse, I start with the above process every time I bridle him and end by helping him finally take the bit by putting my fingers on his tongue or whatever I need to do to finish the skill properly, with the bit in and the bridle on.

Once the bit is in the horse's mouth, I raise it and work the headstall over his ears by raising my right hand. I like to put the right ear under the headstall first because it's easier for me to not scrape the bridle over that right eye if I do the right side first. Then, I can do the left side and see what I'm doing. Try not to fold the horse's ears; just tip them forward one at a time and feed the crown of the headstall over them.

Like everything else in horsemanship, you don't want to over-think this. Some horses will get impatient if you fool around too much. Good bridling should be smooth, efficient, and quiet. Good bridling will end up being invisible. It won't be flashy, and it won't take a long time, but it will feel good between the two of you. It's just one of those things that, when done well, only helps your relationship with your horse and further develops your awareness and mindfulness. Like many rituals, we can do this one mindlessly or mindfully, building feel and connection between us and our horse.

To watch a free video of Kathleen bridling a horse in this manner, please visit:

http://www.ethosequine.com/extras

Chapter 9

It Depends...

I used to hate hearing horsemen answer questions with that cryptic little riddle, "It depends." For a long time, it sure sounded like a non-answer to me. After all, questions HAVE to have some kind of answer, don't they? "It depends." What kind of an answer is that???

I suppose as I get older and (hopefully) wiser, certain things become clearer and certain riddles cease to be riddles. After all, a riddle is only a riddle if we don't understand it. And this is one of those. It's a riddle until it makes sense. Then, it becomes a truth, a "saying," a cliché, a belief, something other than a riddle.

I think I'm just getting to the place where "It depends" isn't so much of a riddle any more. Let me tell you why.

Some time ago, when I was riding in a roping clinic, the teacher didn't have a lot of time to bring us greenhorns along, so he kept things pretty basic. Roping can be very dangerous, so a lot of what he helped us with was learning to be safe in a roping pen with our horses, the stock, and each other.

On day two, the teacher told me, "Now, it's going to sound like I'm contradicting myself, but I'm not. You have to use common sense here. I told you never to let the rope between you and the thing you roped touch the ground. That's true. But if I'm on the heels of a steer and he's kicking the snot out of the guy on the ground, I'm probably going to ride right up there and leave all my slack on the ground so I can get up there quick and help that guy out. So, I've given you some rules, but you have to use your common sense at all times."

About the same time, I heard this advice again from another teacher. This teacher was starting some colts with his students. I can't tell you how many times he pointed out adjustments he was making for this colt and that colt and why. Some colts you can cinch one way, and other colts you might want to cinch another way. Some colts can be touched one way, and others are going to need to be touched some other way. This teacher was also very clear that how we work with a colt is different from how we work with a grown-up horse with a good knowledge-base. With a colt, we want to set it up and wait. We don't want to scare him. We want to build his confidence in us. With a grown-up horse, we can hurry him some and insist that he do what he knows how to do when we ask him to do it, but if we do that with a colt, we could blow him up. So, again, "it depends."

I got to thinking about that pretty hard — about how much we all just want an A+B=C recipe for our work with our horses, and we want a hard and fast set of rules to follow. That would make all this so much easier. Tell me what's "right," tell me what's "wrong," and I'll embrace the "right" and avoid the "wrong." Simple, right?

Well, it just doesn't work that way with horses. There are just too many variables. Think about it. In scientific studies, what scientists try to do is reduce the number of variables so that causation can be proven. In other words, for something to be provable and for that proof to have credibility, there can't be too many variables in the study. Scientists want to be able to prove that when they changed "X," it caused "Y" to happen. If we change "X" and "A" and "M" and "Q," we can't say which one caused "Y" to happen. One of the things that drives scientifically-minded people crazy about horses is the number of variables that influence even the most mundane decisions.

What we could do in any given situation to help the horse or get a change from them might depend on the horse's age, the horse's size, the horse's previous training, the horse's history, the horse's temperament, the horse's conformation, the rider/handler's age, size, strength, skill, experience, timing, whether they're wearing a helmet or not, what kind of boots they're wearing, what footing conditions the work is being done on, whether the horse is shod or barefoot, what kind of tack is being used, the weather that day, the lighting, the geography of the work area, whether there are other people/horses present in the work area, how much time is available, and on and on and on. The mother of all variables are how the horse is responding in that moment and how the person is responding in that moment. So, I don't see how we can deny the truth of "it depends."

Of course, that doesn't make it seem any less overwhelming. But it's really not. If we are a beginner or an intermediate horse person, we should be learning the rules and the generalizations that will soon turn into "it depends." If we are an advanced horse person, then we are usually working in the realm of "it depends," and we need to get as good as we can get at that.

Let's look at my roping again. I am a beginner roper, so I'm going to spend a lot of time learning general skills and the "rules." I'm (hopefully) not going to be in situations where I'm going to have to exercise exceptions to the rules, so I should have some time in my roping learning curve to master those general rules. When I know the rules and I own them in my work, then I can start using my common sense to make exceptions to those rules and begin working in the realm of "it depends."

It's also a lot like English. There are tons of rules in the English language, and it seems like most of them have exceptions. In the beginning, we have to learn the rules, and we spend all our time mastering the rules. It's only after we've mastered the rules that we can explore why we might make exceptions to the rules (think e.e. cummings!). We don't want to break a rule out of ignorance. We want to break a rule out of common sense or, knowingly, to achieve a goal.

We can learn more than one way to do the things we're doing. We can learn the rules. We can own them. Then, we can use common sense to deliberately and intentionally break the "rules" if that's what's called for. Is "it depends" frustrating? Sure, it is. But, anymore, when I hear a horseman say, "Well... now... it depends..." my ears perk up because I know something good is coming.

Chapter 10

If We Quit, We Can't Help

Years ago, I did a fall clinic in Ballston Spa, New York, and while there, I met the head starter from Saratoga Race Track. Bob Duncan was kind enough to introduce himself after lunch one day as I gathered my horse for the afternoon's work. I sensed a passionate enthusiasm in Bob, and we had a short but pretty sophisticated discussion about horsemanship while I saddled my horse. Bob told me he was the "head starter" at Saratoga, and based on my (minimal) knowledge at the time, I assumed that he had something to do with the starting gate.

Bob and I got to talk some more while I was in town, and I got to hear his story. I do hope he'll forgive me if I get any of it sideways. Bob grew up as a second-generation New York Racing Association starter. His father was a starter, and Bob followed in his footsteps. One day, like many of us, Bob woke up and wondered why he was hurting horses. He gave it a lot of thought. Then, he went looking for help. He found Pat Parelli and Monty Roberts, met up with them, listened, worked, and asked questions.

Then, he went back to his job on the track. He changed things at the starting gate. He trained his staff to do things in ways that would make things better for the horses. He became very respected for his effectiveness. He became the guy who hands out "gate cards" and decides which horses do the starting gate safely enough to race. He got called in on Kentucky Derby day and became a consultant to the NYRA. If anyone has a gate problem with a race horse, they call Bob.

I watched Bob and his crew work on a rainy, sloppy day in October at the Oklahoma Track, Saratoga's training track. Bob and three other guys were on duty from 7:30 am to 10:00 am to be available to work with young Thoroughbreds at the starting gate. Each horse's trainer must tell the exercise rider to visit the gate crew as part of that day's training. Some trainers do, some don't. Some days are busy, some aren't. Gate crews have one of the most dangerous jobs on the track. They wear helmets and body protectors.

I'd never been at the gate before at a track, much less witness to "morning exercise." As we waited for Bob, my friend, Frieda, and I watched exercise riders cross a busy Saratoga city street sitting on young, well-fed Thoroughbred colts and fillies that didn't stop or steer. I started thinking that my job was pretty tame. Some riders had their hands full; others slouched in the saddle on quiet youngsters.

Bob took us back to the gate and got out his clip board. On his board, he recorded each horse's name after it worked the gate, as well as what they did with it. He had pages and pages of records. A rider would ride up, and one of the gate crew would hook a lead strap to the bit. Then, they would ask the horse to stop, come forward, and back up. Then, they might approach the gate. Many of the horses simply walked into the stall and then backed out and went on about their morning work. Others had the front gates opened and calmly walked out. No one broke at speed.

A couple of the horses were clearly troubled by the gate. Or maybe the gate was just part of their troubles. These horses were taken aside by Bob's crew, and then they started at the end stall, a wider stall with no front gates on it. I was struck by how troubled these horses were. Steam and sweat poured off them, and they weren't "working." There was a lot of anxiety there for those horses. Their muscles were rigid; their eyes looked far away. They didn't want to be there.

To be fair, I've seen that look before — in show horses, in trail horses, and in backyard horses. The track has no corner on that look.

I was also struck by how accurate the releases that Bob and his crew gave were. Before they took each horse to the gate, they had him do a bit of simple ground work: stop, back, come forward, look at me. They petted the horses and stroked them. I saw horsemanship there at the gate that morning. Those horses looked to Bob and his calm, quiet energy there at the gate. He was the quiet place for them to be. It was palpable.

I saw a bunch of horses at Saratoga who were totally fine with their jobs. They looked like ranch horses look on a ranch, "Ho hum, this is what we do every day..." I also saw some horses who hated it and wished they were anywhere else, but there was Bob and his crew, helping them for two minutes at a time.

We went out for coffee about halfway through the morning, during a particularly heavy down pour, and Bob pointed at the barns and the track and the grandstands. "This will always be here," he said. "People will race horses. People need these jobs."

That was a huge moment for me. Bob didn't quit. He woke up one morning and wondered why he was doing what he was doing. Then, he figured it out. Racing was going to happen. He could quit and ensure that he'd have no positive impact as racing went on without him, or he could work hard and try to make what difference he could for the horses he came in contact with. And that's what he's done. And he's got a crew that's doing the same. Bob wants the starting gate to be the best place a horse can go on the track. That's the idea.

I learned a few really important things from Bob in those short hours. I learned that we don't make things better for the horses by quitting. I learned that we (as a community) don't have a right to judge what we haven't seen. We can't judge a community by what we see on the nightly news or hear on the street. We can say that we hate racing or hate the Tennessee Walker business or whatever our pet peeve is. And that's fine. It's easy to judge from a distance and make no real impact. Or, like Bob, we can learn more, stay involved, and make a real difference in our small sphere of influence. I also learned that anyone contemplating taking on an off-the-track Thoroughbred as a riding horse should spend a day at the track so that they understand where their horse is coming from. I own one, and I understand better now.

It's been a hard road for Bob. Every year, he takes part in a clinic in Kentucky where he and other clinicians help career track workers do their jobs better. When Bob first discovered a "different" way of doing things, he was on fire. He couldn't imagine that others wouldn't be as interested and excited as he was. He said he looked out on 125 faces at a clinic, and saw 124 blank stares. But he saw one light bulb go on out there. At first he was flabbergasted at the poor attendance-to-conversion ratio. Then he began to see that that's how any of us make a difference – one person and one horse at a time.

We can't quit. But we also can't expect to convert the masses. We can't be frustrated by that. Good horsemanship is good horsemanship, whether anyone sees it or jumps on the bandwagon or not. We're lucky to have each other.

Chapter 11

On "Natural Horsemanship"

I think I first came across this term around about 1994, give or take a couple of years. At the time, I had been a lifelong horse person and rider, but I'd had a stroke. Unsurprisingly, I had quite a bit of trouble with the horse I bought right after my stroke. The internet was fairly new then, but it gave me the opportunity to get exposed to some things that I wouldn't have stumbled across otherwise. It didn't hurt that about that time I also moved to Colorado, which has had a very strong horse culture for a long time.

Back then, clinics were already happening, and there were lots in Colorado. On the internet, online discussions took the form of clunky email services that sent "dumps" of messages once a day. It was very awkward and clumsy, but I think many of us learned a lot from those slow back-and-forth horsemanship discussions. "Clinic reports" were a "thing" that basically provided a play-by-play report about any clinic you cared to look into. I lurked enthusiastically back then, because, to be honest, I had no idea what people were talking about. I was a sponge. I read the discussions hungrily, understanding only a fraction of the content. I devoured clinic reports and subscribed to *The Trail Less Traveled* magazine (precursor to *Eclectic Horseman*).

What we had in common, back then, was our interest in "natural horsemanship." At the time, I could not have cared less what it was called, I just knew that I had to find another way to be with horses, because what I knew how to do and how to be was no longer working. Knowing what it was called just helped me find teachers, information, and resources (and friends!).

Since then, the term has kind of been "rode hard and put away wet," hijacked, overused, misused, and just plain worn the heck out. My understanding, way back then, was simply that the term denoted ways of working with horses that were based on respecting the fact that the horse is a herd and a prey animal. For me, having come from a world of show horses, this was quite revolutionary. I'd actually never thought about horses that way before. Though I'd been in the horse world for decades (as a child rider, then a junior exhibitor, then an amateur exhibitor, and finally as a professional trainer and instructor), I really had no idea what made horses tick. If a horse said "no" to me, about the only thing I had in my toolbox was literally a stick to hit him with. I don't know that I'd ever even questioned WHY a horse might say "no."

But, there's kind of an obvious problem with this term, "natural horsemanship," even if it wasn't worn out and out of use at the time of this writing. There's really nothing "natural" about fencing a horse in, selectively breeding him, strapping dead cow hides to him, and riding him. So "natural" is kind of a funny thing to call it anyway.

There was a period of time when the term temporarily seemed to mean "all things natural" horsemanship, so people went barefoot, blanket-less, treeless, bitless, and vaccine-less. I guess we found our "natural" somewhere else even though the horse was still fenced in and selectively bred.

It's really kind of too bad that the term is dead. I'd really like more horse people to be reminded that horses are herd and prey animals. It seems to me that this lack of awareness is at the root of most of the problems we have with horses ~ that they're herd and prey animals, and those things can take them far away from being a trail horse or a show horse or a "bombproof" family horse. Their herd and prey animal-ness makes their horsey lives pretty difficult a lot of the time. It wouldn't be a problem for them at all if they didn't have to live in this human world.

It's also important to remember that not everything that went on with horses previous to the popularization of the term "natural horsemanship" was horrible. Every era of history has seen gifted, compassionate, and innovative horsemen. Some wrote books and taught and shared what they knew, while others just did their work with integrity in obscure places with obscure horses. We're not reinventing the wheel here. Xenophon wrote one of the first treatises on "natural horsemanship" in 350 B.C. (that is, Before Christ). Think about that a bit. Our interest in good horsemanship pre-dates CHRIST. So, this stuff has been around for a while, and it's not a new idea or a new movement, really. It's been out there for a very, very, long time.

I find that comforting, on the one hand, and discouraging on the other. It's comforting because we're not really trying to do something that hasn't been done before. There are resources and teachers out there. There's a track record and a history. There are people whose tracks we can follow, and we don't need to "reinvent the wheel," so to speak. On the discouraging side, even though "enlightened" types of horsemanship have been around for SO long, they continue to be the horse community's "last resort," when all the "conventional" or "main stream" approaches aren't working. Most folks really have to get to the end of their rope to give this stuff a try. Though it's been around since before Christ, and though it has a track record and a proven success rate, it's rarely a horse person's first choice of technique or philosophy.

But we'll keep after it, advocating for the horse and who he is. Historically, we are in good company.

Chapter 12

....

On Starting at the Beginning Rather Than at the End

For centuries, humankind has found it important to order thin-gs — to put first things first, second things second, and last things last, so to speak. Stories have a beginning, middle, and end. In school, we learn how to organize our thoughts in outli-ne form from the largest, most general ideas to the smallest and most specific. Creatures in our world are organized by kingdom, phylum, class, order, family, genus, and, finally, species. In martial arts, one starts as a white belt and progresses through the levels of skill in a rational manner, earning each new belt by proving proficiency at one's present belt level. One learns to play piano in an orderly way, starting with scales, fingering, and simple tunes, rather than jumping off with a masterwork by Handel or Bach.

It's natural for people to want to put things in order, and it's really pretty rational since it's often essential to put things in their proper order so that they work correctly. A house must be built in a particular order; obviously, we can't put the roof on until it's framed, and we can't do the finish work if it's not sheetrocked.

So, anyone who builds houses is an expert at putting things in a logical order.

There is also a logical order to learning to ride and work with horses. There are certain skills and pieces of knowledge that you must have before you can build upon them. And I'm not quite sure how it's happened, but it seems like many of today's riders and horsemen have kind of lost sight of this fact. In some cases, we're trying to kind of start at the end, or at the middle, and we're getting frustrated and perhaps even injured as a result.

Maybe this has something to do with the fact that most of today's clinic-goers are women who are returning to horses after decades away. Maybe the long break that some of us have taken has interrupted the order in our equestrian education, and by the time we get back into it, our dreams have overtaken reality.

This wouldn't be a big deal except that when we try to start at the end, it's the horse who pays for it. The person becomes frustrated, and then the horse has to work with an unstable, emotionally-charged rider who is not making rational decisions. Or, we end up leaving "holes" in ourselves or the horse as we hurry past steps that are "boring" or don't seem very important right now.

Trying to start at the end can look lots of different ways. It can look like a beginner or intermediate horseman buying a troubled or remedial horse. It can look like a lower-level rider wondering why they have so few "magic moments" with their horse and thinking that means they're doing something wrong. It can look like the rider falling off a lot and getting injured riding the horse they "love." It can look like a rider being frustrated that their horse can't collect, while the rider is using the horse's mouth for balance. It can look like asking a young horse for high levels of "collection" because we've never ridden a green horse before and don't understand the process by which the skill of collection is built.

So, let's look at this as a matter of order. When one is a beginner in any sport or hobby, we start at a beginner level. We have a bigger tennis racket, and the coach lobs those balls pretty slow. Baseball players start with T-ball, then softball, then baseball.

So, a beginner/intermediate rider needs a beginner/intermediate-appropriate horse so that they can learn all the things beginner/intermediate riders need to learn. A beginner/intermediate rider with an advanced horse may miss the opportunity to learn all of the beginner/intermediate things that advanced things are built on.

Learning to have an independent seat is so important, and this is missing in many riders today. By "independent seat," I mean that the rider's seat, legs, and body are balanced and independent from the hands and that the rider is not using their hands and the horse's mouth for balance or to stay on. Because many of today's riders have not had an orderly riding education, the independent seat has been missed. Now, lessons are not the only way to learn an independent seat; many of us learned to have an independent seat by tearing around the countryside bareback for years as kids. We fell off a lot. But we learned.

It is only when we have an independent seat that we can use our cues or aids (from thoughts, visualizations, and breathing to hands, legs, and seat) in a subtle and sympathetic way with feel and timing. As long as we are using our reins for balance, there is little subtlety. This is part of the order to things when it comes to learning to ride and work with a horse.

I think that we get frustrated when we violate the order of things because our expectations and wishes are beyond what our knowledge or ability level will support.

My ex-husband was an avid and athletic outdoorsman in the Colorado Rockies. He would get up at 5am to "skin" up Aspen's ski mountains and then ski down before the mountains opened to the public for the day. He could mountain bike amazing terrain and hike 4,000 vertical feet straight up Aspen Mountain. I remember he used to complain of what he called "gear heads." These were people who had gone out and bought all the gear, good gear, and thought that buying the gear gave them the skill to use it. "Having the gear doesn't give you the skill. Working at it gives you the skill," he said. He was seeing people who were trying to start at the end, and they were failing and frustrating themselves and others in the process.

I've thought about that a lot since then — about how we become "gear heads" in the horse world. If we buy the horse, the tack, the trailer, and whatnot, we have just begun, not ended. Now, we can put in the hours of practice and preparation, and if we do things in a rational order, we should get positive results of some sort. If our expectations match our skill and knowledge level, we can be happy where we are — maybe not satisfied, but pretty darn happy.

Every level of every skill has something to offer us. They are really ONLY focused on at that level. If we skip them then, we may not get to circle back to them unless their absence causes us to wreck or fail in some way and a wise advisor has enough influence over us to cause us to BACKTRACK and make up what we've missed. That's why it's important that we're honest about the level we're at right now, that we understand what skills comprise that level, and that we don't advance until those skills have been mastered. This is when it may be important to have a trusted friend, peer, or instructor who will level with us about where we are and who we will listen to when they tell us the truth.

We need not be ashamed of where we are in our journey. Instead, we could be thinking about milking every last drop out of each level we inhabit and only moving on when we've "got all the good out of it."

Chapter 13

The Long Walk

I see myself as a horseman. I hope I am one, but maybe I'm not, yet. So, let's just say that I aspire to be a horseman. To me, horsemanship is defined as the *art* of riding, working with, caring for, and having a relationship with the horse. A horseman studies that art. But, unfortunately, this is not all unicorns and rainbows. Perhaps one of the more uncomfortable aspects of being a horseman is playing god.

This is the part of horsemanship that requires us to decide when one of our equine partners dies, when we decide the last day of that horse's life. I think if we're a horseman, that's part of the deal. If we have one or more of these fantastic creatures in our lives, we need to be prepared to make that most difficult of decisions — to end that animal's life. Anything can happen, and things don't always go to plan.

This is a tough subject, and you may not agree with me on a philosophical level. That's okay. This is about personal philosophy and personal responsibility. I wish this subject wasn't part of the deal, but it is. This is the world we've volunteered to live in. If we own a horse, we may have to play god someday.

Like any other crisis that we know might hit us, like wild fires, hurricanes, floods, or tornadoes, we need to have a crisis plan. When we're in the middle of the crisis is not the time to try to develop the plan because we won't be thinking straight. That's why we need to have that plan in place ahead of time so that we can just follow it.

The same is true in a horse care crisis. We need to know what we consider to be the maximum dollar amount that we can spend to save each horse we own. We need to know if they're a good patient or not. We need to know how long we're willing to work toward getting the horse sound or healthy. We need to know how far it is to our best local surgical facility and how to get a horse in there (it's usually by referral). We need to have transportation to said facility, and our horse needs to know how to load, even under stress. We need to know if we were to put a horse down, where we would do it and who we would ask to help us. I'm here to tell you that you likely won't be able to do it on your own, so plan to have supportive, non-judgmental friends who you can call and who will drop everything to help you. Discuss this with them so they understand what will be needed. Have a plan. I hope you'll never need to use it.

A few years ago, it was baby Henry who took the long walk, out to the oak grove, where he now lies beneath the sand.

Henry was my first and only (to date) baby horse that I bred myself. I had a lovely Dutch Warmblood mare, Ruby, who was not very sound because of her career as a show horse. I used her lightly in my clinic business for a few years and then decided that she might provide me with a nice cross-bred baby.

I booked her to a colored Thoroughbred stallion, but she struggled to conceive using cooled semen. My repro vet took pity on us and offered to breed her to his paint stallion. After meeting the stallion, I accepted his offer, and she was bred to the vet's stallion.

Ruby took with twins, and the vet pinched one. I joked later that he pinched the colored filly, because Henry was born a plain bay colt. Henry was born uneventfully while I was on the road, and I had a great time weaning and halter breaking him when my clinic schedule was done for the year.

The details of Henry's Long Walk are not important, but suffice it to say that (what looked like) a tiny little scrape turned out to be a horribly aggressive infection of his hock joint. When my vet, Nicole, looked at the hock the first time and took his temperature, she looked at the thermometer and said, "How much do you love this horse?"

As prepared as I'd schooled myself to be in the event of this kind of crisis, preparation didn't make it easy. That's why I feel it's important for us to talk about this. A good horseman is prepared and does what needs to be done for the good of the horse. What's good for the horse may or may not be good for us. That's why we need to be prepared. Emotion and stress will muddy the data coming to us in those moments. It's somewhere between difficult and impossible to think straight, but life and death hangs in the balance.

In Baby Henry's case, time was ticking as well. The longer his hock was infected, the slimmer his chances were. If we were going to try surgery and heavy-duty antibiotics, he had to go the next day. Time was not on our side.

I spent a long, sleepless night tossing and turning and running through scenarios in my mind. I checked bank and credit card balances so that I knew what I was dealing with. In the morning, I gathered more information by talking to my local vet again and then talking to the surgeon at the regional hospital facility. Then, I went back and looked at the numbers again, forwards, backwards, and sideways. I did all the math a dozen times. When all the information had come in, it was clear that Henry's prognosis for future "quality of life" was poor, at best, and nonexistent, at worst, no matter how much money I spent, if I even had it to spend, which I did not. Once I had the information I needed, the decision kind of made itself.

I bred this colt. I brought him into this world, on purpose. I had anticipated his arrival for months and months. I cherished him and dreamed about his future. I indulged in dreams about his "potential." And now I was going to take him out of this world, on purpose. I couldn't see any other way that was fair to him. The guilt of having brought him **into** the world for my own pleasure was heavy, and it still is.

I'm here as a reminder that as a horse owner and a horseman, you need to be prepared. We can all hope for the best, but we need to prepare for the worst. As guardians of these fantastic creatures, we need to be able do what is best for them, whatever that is. We need to be prepared to play god. If we're really horsemen, we will make a decision that's best for the horse, even if it's not best for us.

We need to develop our disaster-preparedness plan and stick to it. We need to take responsibility for the lives in our care. We need to ready ourselves for whatever may happen, including the unthinkable or unlikely, so that we can still function if the time comes. Our horses need us to be able to do this.

When Henry got hurt, I was so very fortunate to be surrounded by supportive, non-judgmental friends. I remember my vet saying, "Whatever you decide, Kathleen, it will be right." I really needed that right then. I had another friend who offered to take Henry for me and hold the lead rope at the critical moment, when I melted down and just couldn't do it. I'd suggest that you have someone like that on call. Talk it through ahead of time so that when it comes to it, all you'll have to say to that friend is, "I need you; it's time." You don't need to explain yourself or the situation in that moment.

"Horses," according to a friend of mine, "will break your heart and feed your soul." She is absolutely right; I have no doubt. And I don't know that it's fair to ask them to do the one and not the other. It just doesn't seem to work that way.

"We who choose to surround ourselves with lives even more temporary than our own, live within a fragile circle, easily and often breached. Unable to accept its awful gaps, we would still live no other way."
~Irving Townsend

Chapter 14

On Being a Good Student

Not long ago, I attended a horsemanship clinic as a spectator, and I was surprised to see how many of the participants struggled with simple learning skills. It seemed to me that a lot of people were going to leave that clinic having learned very little at all, and from what I saw, it was the participants themselves who were mostly responsible for that. I was surprised that someone would come all that way and pay all that money and then just blatantly and rudely disregard the instruction being offered.

I got to thinking about that right then and there, and I jotted down some notes about how some of those students could perhaps have gotten out of their own way better. I thought I'd share those notes here. This is not an exhaustive list of hints and tips for how to be a good student. Rather, it's just some of the observations I made as a spectator (and student). My hope is that some of these ideas might help each of us on our own paths as students.

a.   Do not talk back to your instructor. Do not argue with them, do not contradict them, and avoid defensive and disrespectful body postures, such as rolling your eyes, crossing your arms across your chest, and standing with your hands on your hips.

b. Do not respond to your teacher with sentences that begin with the words "but" or "if".

c. Do not speak when your instructor is talking. Practice active listening.

d. Try your hardest to do what your instructor is asking you to do. If you fail, let it not be because you didn't try, but just because you cannot do it...yet.

e. Buy the best instruction you can afford.

f. Help your instructor teach you well. Know how you learn best and what your learning style is, and understand that if a teacher's teaching style doesn't match your learning style, it may be on you to work that out.

g. Learn to quiet yourself inside. It's hard to get anything into a vessel that is already full.

h. Respect your teacher. Do not choose or stay with an instructor you cannot or do not respect and want to listen to. If you cannot or will not respect your teacher, it's time to either get a new teacher or change your attitude.

i. Observe the basic rules of polite conversation with your instructor. Say, "excuse me," to gain their attention, thank them for answering your questions, and acknowledge that you've understood their directions. If you are confused or unclear, say so.

j. While you are in a lesson, do what the instructor is asking you to do. If you choose not to follow their instruction in the future, that's fine. But IN THE LESSON, have the respect to attempt their instructions. You didn't pay them to not try what they're offering.

k. A teacher's job is to teach. If a teacher is emotionally volatile, emotionally abusive and/or manipulative, explosive, or unpredictable, a student should have the right to discuss their concerns in private (the teacher may be unaware that they are coming off this way), and, then, depending on the results of that conversation, the student can vote with their feet, as they say. The relationship between a teacher and a student should not be "toxic."

And spectators, you have a different list of things to think about:

a. BE QUIET. Do not talk on your phone or carry on conversations in the audience. Speaking while the instructor is teaching is very disrespectful, and they can hear you doing it.

b. Do NOT wish bad things to happen to participants so that you can have fun watching. Energy is energy, and YOUR energy influences what happens in the arena!

c. Do not talk about what you would do differently or SO much better than those in the arena. Pay your money next time and show us.

d. Ask questions respectfully, and thank the teacher for answering your questions. Do not ask questions in such a way that your question is clearly a poorly-veiled criticism of a participant.

e. After the clinic, thank the participants for allowing you to learn from their experience (and money), and say something nice to them about their horse. They will really appreciate that.

Chapter 15

....

Deliberate Practice

Ioften read books that aren't about horses but that have a profound effect on my horsemanship all the same. A while ago, I started to wonder about the "mystery" of exemplary performance. In other words, I was wondering if some of my students were just "born" with more "talent" for horse work than others. I was looking for some information on how I, as a teacher, could help ensure that all my students moved forward in their horsemanship as much as they could.

Years ago, I read a book called *Blink* by Malcolm Gladwell. That book is about what I would call "unconscious intelligence." In other words, it's a proven fact that we can know more than we think we do. Our "little voice" is often right. I thought that book was really useful for horsemen to read.

Then, a while later, I read a book called *The Talent Code* by Daniel Coyle. The premise of this book is the scientific evidence behind the proposition that talent is not "born" but, instead, "made." Again, I thought this was pretty interesting reading when applied to my job of teaching people to be better with their horses (or teaching horses to be better at things, for that matter).

The Talent Code led me to a book called *Talent Is Overrated* by Geoff Colvin. In this book, I found the concept that helped me actually "give legs" to all of these ideas. In *Talent is Overrated*, Colvin quantifies the kind of practice that tends to create exemplary performance: "deliberate practice." Colvin references the work of Swedish psychologist Anders Ericsson, who originally proposed the elements of deliberate practice. The idea of deliberate practice can help explain why some of us get better over time and some of us don't.

In brief, the elements of deliberate practice are as follows:

1. It is designed specifically to improve performance. Deliberate practice is work that is outside the comfort zone and not yet in the panic zone; it is in the learning zone — in between the comfort and panic zones. Deliberate practice focuses on things that are difficult or not yet working the way we need them to.

2. Repetition. Malcolm Gladwell proposes that one cannot achieve expert or virtuoso status until at least 10,000 hours of practice have been achieved. Most extraordinary achievers practice around 5 hours a day.

3. Critical feedback on results must be continuously available. Having a teacher or coach point out weaknesses and suggest learning zone activities is key. A teacher or guide can also help design practice (see #1).

4. Deliberate practice is incredibly demanding. The combination of repetition, operating in the learning zone, and focusing on weak links in one's performance means that deliberate practice can be exhausting.

5. This is the kicker. Deliberate practice IS NOT MUCH FUN. Add #1-4 above, and it's not exactly a recipe for daily "mountaintop moments."

For me, the takeaway here is that the kind of practice that is actually going to lead to a measurable improvement in our skill is not the kind of practice that most of us are attracted to, unfortunately. Deliberate practice is hard and tedious, and it doesn't necessarily feel good at the time or immediately afterward. Think of Michael Jordan shooting free throws after practice until bed time or Tiger Woods working sand trap shots by dropping a ball in the sand and then stepping on it before practicing the shot.

How many of us do that kind of practice in our horse work? How many of us are content to do the same one hour of (non-deliberate) practice over and over for years? That's how we end up with "one year of experience 20 times" rather than 20 years of experience with horses.

Deliberate practice can be tough, for several reasons. First, we may not have identified WHAT exactly we personally need to practice. We may need an objective third person to help with that. We may find we don't have the confidence to operate (especially unsupervised) in the learning zone, so we end up in our comfort zone over and over again. The fear of practicing "wrong" can also drive us back to our comfort zone. Or, we simply may not have time for the repetition that deliberate practice requires. We may not be emotionally and mentally resilient enough to focus on our weaknesses and "get it wrong" until we "get it right."

Think of it this way, deliberate practice looks like someone picking up, say, a fiddle, and starting to play a piece they're learning. Let's say they get three measures into the piece, and they make a mistake. They stop playing the piece right there and may repeat the note that caused the problem or the phrase that included the problem over and over again until they easily get it correct. Then, they start the piece over from the beginning again. Each time they stumble over a note, or a rest, or a transition, or a fingering, they stop right there and practice until it's better. This might happen many, many times in one piece of music.

We horse people COULD practice like that, but many of us don't tend to. Lots of times, when we "stub our toe" on something with our horse, we keep moving right along rather than stop and practice that spot until it's better and then start over from the beginning, like that piece of music in the fiddle analogy. So, over time, more and more things add up until "out of nowhere" our horse has become untrained, and some of the skills that are tripping us up aren't getting any better. In the horse world, this lack of the kind of practice we'd use to learn to play an instrument is rampant, as far as I can see. We do a lot of getting it "good enough" (whatever that means) and moving on or making up excuses or stories to get out of practicing ("My horse has done that since I got him," or "He was abused, so I just let him do that."). What would happen if we actually got our horse working BETTER than we'll ever need them to? What if we could load our horse while sitting on the fender of the trailer? What if we had the self-discipline to practice deliberately?

For those of us who truly want to move forward in our horse work, toward some degree of not only competence but also mastery, I think it could be helpful to study the tenants of deliberate practice. According to contemporary thought, talent is not the game of chance that some of us once thought it was, and I find that to be exciting news. I hope those of you who consider yourselves serious students of horsemanship will find joy in the tedious but necessary work that will improve your horsemanship. I will be right there with you.

Chapter 16

···

The Hearst Castle and Horsemanship

Okay, stick with me on this one.

On our honeymoon in 2013, Glenn and I headed over to the central California coast to hang out, visit wineries, and otherwise just kick around and relax. One of the places we visited is known as Hearst Castle, which is a 65,000 square-foot residence built by media mogul William Randolph Hearst and architect Julia Morgan between about 1919 and 1947. Today, it is run as a tourist attraction by the State of California, having been gifted to the state by the Hearst family.

The Castle is, of course, a study in excess and opulence. Hearst was clearly influenced by his childhood visits to European castles, and the building is filled with ancient furniture and artifacts that he brought over from Europe. The fireplaces are big enough for an adult to walk into upright, the ceilings soar to 20 feet and more, and the walls are covered with centuries-old wood paneling and tapestries. It has 38 bedrooms, 30 fireplaces, 42 bathrooms, and 14 sitting rooms. It's a heck of a thing to see, to be sure.

All that's fine and dandy, but let's get to the horsemanship part of this. Hearst Castle is built of poured concrete. If Hearst was going to bother to build this, I guess he figured he wanted it to be as earthquake-proof as possible. At that time, poured concrete was a bit cutting-edge as a building material. Keep in mind that where the Castle is situated at the time it was built, it was five miles and 1600 vertical feet from the nearest road. When the building was started, they had no automobiles, so all this concrete was hauled in, mixed by hand, and dumped into the forms BY HAND. Looking at this massive monolith, it's really pretty unbelievable.

But Hearst Castle has stood the test. In 2003, a large earthquake centered not far from the estate rocked the building, but when inspected later, no structural damage was found. That's 70 years after it was built, which is more than a little impressive.

When Glenn and I toured Hearst Castle, we walked up and down some large spiral staircases where we could still see the rough marks from the wood used to construct the forms into which the concrete was poured. One of the members of our tour asked if these plain, slightly ugly, and rough staircases would have been used by the Castle's guests. Indeed, said our guide. These staircases were it. Mr. Hearst had not thought it was important to finish out the staircases. Those staircases were an important glimpse into the foundation, the basic "bones" if you will, of that building. In the other rooms, the rough concrete had been covered with silk, ancient wood panels, paintings, or tapestries. But the staircases told the truth. The pretty stuff was just that—pretty stuff. It wasn't the pretty stuff that kept that building standing in an earthquake.

To me, the Hearst Castle is a great metaphor for how I see horsemanship. That foundation is what we rely on in a crisis. If we have no foundation, no poured concrete, so to speak, we likely won't fare well in a crisis. That goes for both us and the horse. If our horse doesn't know how to function in the real world (the human world) or we don't have, for example, an independent seat, good luck to us.

The foundation of Hearst Castle wasn't pretty. It wasn't spectacular. The people who poured it are not famous. Just like people who help horses with their foundations, they didn't get any fanfare for doing it. Those are the horse trainers in the background, doing their thing, day in and day out, saving horses lives and enabling them to bring joy to untold people with no awards and no fame and fortune. They're not the people in the limelight earning the big money. They're the folks working for equine minimum wage on the sides of mountains and out in the back woods so that someone else can get the credit for putting the pretty finishing touches on later.

This is a good place to consider the question, "What constitutes a good foundation in a horse?" I think my own answer to this will evolve and change as my work does the same, but I've given this a LOT of thought over the years. I have come to see, over time, how important a horse's foundation is, so I started to ask myself, "What matters and what doesn't?"

The stuff I'm going to talk about here doesn't have anything to do with disciplines or breeds. The foundation is at the "bottom" of a horse, and other breed- or discipline-specific stuff gets layered on top. So, as I see it, the foundational requirements for any horse are pretty much the same.

These aren't in an order of importance because they're all equally important. However, it sometimes makes the most sense to put these in a certain order when working with a horse, so then order would become important. This stuff isn't about teaching a horse "tricks" or repetitive behaviors. It's more about teaching broad concepts that the horse can generalize to the rest of his life as he matures and, eventually, works at a job.

I think it's important for a horse to be friendly toward people (have some "reach" in him, we could say) and at the same time understand safe personal boundaries around people. I'd like him to understand when energy in the environment has something to do with him (is a cue) and when it doesn't have anything to do with him. He needs to be able to separate these from each other. I want the horse to be soft and yielding to the halter yet able to follow a feel in the rope. I want the lead rope to have meaning and to be connected to the horse's feet and, through them, his mind. I want the horse to be soft and yielding to a rope on any of his feet. I want him to be able to have his feet picked up with the rope, and I want him to lead by his feet and stop by a rope on his foot. I want him to understand the concept of restraint without his feet getting stuck. It's important that he understands how to tie and have patience. I want him to be good around other horses and be able to be off by himself. I want him to have balance.

And, what, you may ask, does all this have to do with the average horse owner? It has a lot to do with the average horse owner. If our horse has missing pieces or misunderstandings in his foundation, he could be anxious, troubled, aggressive, spooky, difficult, "quirky," worried, etc., and he could even have soundness and other physical issues. He's like a person who's in way over their head at work—which is really stressful. If you're way in over your head at work, you're going to fail. It's inevitable. Because you don't have the tools for the job.

We, the average horse owner, have the ability to help our horses with their foundation, but not everyone is going to be up to this challenge. Foundation work is often tedious and boring. Sometimes it's hard to tell if you're getting anywhere. It often looks like nothing's happening. It's not a "fast and feel-good" kind of thing, which is probably why more people don't focus on it. It's more the kind of thing where we wake up one day and realize we have a new horse in the pasture, and we can hardly remember all the trouble we had with the old one. The average horse owner can do this work. And when we do, we will learn feel and timing, and we will build something with our horse that will last a lifetime. We need to keep that in mind—that a foundation lasts a lifetime, be it good, bad, or indifferent. If we share a foundation with our horse, we always have somewhere to go, some previous understanding we can refer to when things get a little sideways. And if we have a good foundation, we have the ability to build amazing levels of refinement.

If none of that fires you up, that's okay. Try thinking of it this way. The first time someone showed me how to change a tire on my car, I thought that, well, that's all fine and good, but I have AAA roadside service, a husband, and a brand-new car. Yup.

And then, one day, there I was, in a snowy canyon in Colorado, by myself with no cell service and a flat tire on my brand-new car. And I knew how to fix it. I had been empowered to help myself and get things working again because I'd been shown how it all fit together and how to use the tools. This is like that except with horses. If you know how it all fits together and how to use the tools, you can help yourself and your horse.

So, now when I look at the horses, I envision the inside of that spiral staircase at Hearst Castle and try to see what that horse has on the inside of his spiral staircases. When we pull the silk back, is there anything there? For me, when I pull back the pretty stuff, I want to see earthquake-proof poured concrete. When a crisis comes, it's not the pretty stuff that saves the day; it's the foundation.

Chapter 17

....

A Profound Quandary

I'm going to pose a lot of questions here, but I'm not likely to offer a whole lot of answers. I don't think I've heard this topic publicly discussed much in the horse world, and I get the feeling that we don't really have a way of addressing it in our culture. However, some of us are probably living with this struggle right now, and if we're fortunate enough not to be facing it ourselves, we may know someone who is.

The profound quandary I speak of is the horse in chronic, daily, unmitigated pain (and if it's mitigated, the horse is just in "less" pain, but still in pain). I think we all agree that horses are "sentient" beings, meaning that they are conscious, aware, and capable of sensation. Basically, that means that horses can feel pain. I believe that a majority (but not all) of horse owners/horsemen agree on this. If we agree that horses CAN feel pain, then I think we subsequently have to agree that horses can display problems (including training issues) because they're in pain and that they can experience CHRONIC (meaning "constant") pain. I suppose the question I'm posing here is this: What, if anything, can and/or should we do about a horse experiencing this kind of pain?

Assessing pain in horses is tricky, mainly because horses can't talk or put their degree of pain on a numerical scale (0-10) like humans can. They also can't point to "where it hurts" like people do. Different horses can display pain in different ways. Some horses are stoic, while others are very dramatic in their expression of pain. Does that mean the stoic horse is in less pain than the dramatic horse?

Then, there's the variable caused by the fact that different people observe and assess equine pain in different ways. At this time, this is a subjective judgment. Researchers are currently working on standardized ways to judge pain in horses, but even so, two people could look at the same horse and come up with completely different numbers on the pain scale.

Veterinarians do not have a standardized methodology to assess and grade pain in horses. They are taught to judge lameness via a head bob and only at the trot, but a horse who is lame on two or four legs will not display a head bob, and some horses display their pain at gaits other than a trot. Does this mean the horse is not "lame"? Does it mean the horse is not in pain? I don't know that there is currently a sure way to diagnose chronic pain (especially full-body pain) in horses.

In my experience so far, not all horses experiencing chronic pain ALSO show a distinct single-legged clinical lameness. Because of this, sadly, a horse in generalized chronic pain without a one-legged lameness can often go unnoticed and undiagnosed.

We assume that horses are born perfect. We assume horses are born sound. But studies show that a surprising percentage of foals are born with rib cage injuries from the birthing process that are severe enough to be visible on an X-ray. Horses are born with crooked legs; why not crooked spines? We assume that all horses have perfect genetics, though they may have the same grandfather on the top and bottom of their papers. Is Seattle Slew on your Thoroughbred's papers? Seattle Slew was a "wobbler" and had a "basket" surgery to stabilize his neck as a young horse. We assume that the huge bones and muscles of the body are impervious to injury because the diagnostics for those areas aren't readily available, and the horse's body is so bulky that diagnostics are very difficult. Again, there are more questions here than there are answers.

When I was on the road doing clinics, I started running some numbers. I'd had the opportunity to follow up with some of the horses I'd seen at clinics over the years and hear what happened after they went home. What I found out is that a surprising number of horses I'd seen at clinics appeared to have as-yet undetected or undiagnosed clinical veterinary issues. These issues I saw (some of which I'd been able to identify and some not) included OCD lesions, arthritis, EPM, Lyme disease, various types of clinical lameness, broken bones, gastric ulcers, clinical foot soreness or back soreness, and various neurological disorders like Wobbler syndrome. I estimate that at least 25% of the horses I saw at clinics had clinical veterinary issues that may or may not have had something to do with why the horse was at the clinic or what he was or wasn't capable of doing while he was there. If my eye had been better, that percentage likely would have gone up, not down.

I estimate that another 20-50% of the horses I saw had less severe, "sub-clinical" physical disorders like chiropractic issues (guarding, "stuckness," lack of movement), soft tissue issues (tightness, soreness), saddle fit issues, and foot issues. Sometimes, these issues manifested in an easily visible clinical head-bobbing lameness, but more often than not, these issues showed in the horse as more subtle asymmetries of gait, muscling, or posture or as behavioral issues like cinchiness, grumpiness about grooming, crow-hopping or bucking, reluctance to go forward, rearing, bit chewing, pawing, and even loading issues.

There is another quandary here for the equine professional. Only veterinarians are licensed and legally entitled, in most states, to make a diagnosis or treatment recommendation to a horse owner. This puts the equine professional and the horse owner themselves in a sticky spot, because we are not always able to obtain all the information we need from our veterinarian. Sometimes it takes a team of multiple professionals and practitioners working together to figure out what's going on and what to do about it. It's also important to keep in mind that when we ask anyone but a veterinarian for a diagnosis or treatment recommendation, we may be asking them to break the law.

These are horrible questions to have to ask, and one question begets more questions, but we as a culture need to face the fact that we don't really have a mechanism to ask and then answer these questions. To get us started, here are some of my questions:

⬥ What would cause us to question if our horse is in chronic pain? How can we tell?

⬥ Once we're ready to ask that question, how would we go about diagnosing the horse's degree of pain?

⬥ If the horse is in chronic pain, is it fixable? How long is okay for him to be in pain while we try to fix it?

⬥ Once we know a horse is in chronic pain (if we can know that), how long is it ethically acceptable for him to remain in chronic pain?

⬥ What is the solution for a horse with unfixable chronic pain? Let the horse live in pain? Euthanasia? Life-long painkillers?

⬥ And then there's the "money question". How much is each of us willing/able/obligated to spend to answer the above questions?

Like I said, I've just got more and more questions on this one, not answers. But this is something that every horse owner is responsible for at least thinking about.

Chapter 18

···

Doing Our Time

I grew up in the regional hunter/jumper business in the Midwest. I showed a lot, from the 4-H level to the A-Circuit level. Because I showed a lot, I rode a lot, and I also hung around the barn a lot. I was what they call a "barn rat." I watched, and I listened. I learned the jargon. I memorized how the grooms bandaged the legs and cleaned the tack and how they hung a halter on a stall door. I often hung around hoping to be an extra hand when someone needed it. Occasionally, I'd get tapped to hold a horse for the farrier, and I'd pepper him with questions while no one was paying attention. I got a thrill out of grooms asking me to put a cooler on a hot horse and walk him around until he was cool. I'd check his chest carefully and present him back to the groom when he was JUST the right temperature. A lot of the time, it felt like fooling around, but I was learning.

By the time I was in my late teens, I was working around horses every hour I wasn't at school. About that time, I began getting the same lecture from many different sources. Be prepared to pay your dues, they told me. Don't expect to be handed anything for free. Expect to work your fingers to the bone for every dollar earned or favor granted. Do your time. There's no substitute for hard work. Do the work that needs to be done. Don't expect to skip your way up the ladder.

There were lots of clichés in those lectures, to be sure, but I've thought a lot about them in the years since then. They helped prepare me for the journey that turned out to be my own horsemanship. Do your time. Do the work. Practice. Don't skip things. Know your subject from the bottom up. Those early lectures prepared me for the work I do now.

In Malcolm Gladwell's book *The Outliers*, he explains what many call the "10,000 Hour Rule," which proposes that it takes 10,000 hours of practice to gain a level of mastery in a skill or field. I think this might kind of be what my lecturers were talking about all those years ago. They hadn't put numbers on it, but they sure did say that competence would come with hours spent working on it.

It seems to me that much of the time and money being spent in the horse industry these days is being spent by middle-aged women who have returned to horses after some time away as they pursued their educations, careers, or maybe even raised a family. These women fill the bulk of horsemanship clinics around the country as well as horse show classes in all disciplines and breeds. They buy feed, they buy tack, they buy grooming supplies, and they buy horses. They keep a substantial portion of the equine economy here in the States functioning.

What's interesting about this demographic is how they tend to fare in the quest to collect 10,000 hours of work with horses. For example, I have a student who is a professional and who also has a husband and two small children. She has one horse. She has been involved with horses for over 15 years. This makes her sound very experienced, doesn't it? When she added up her hours, she found she had only 2,500 hours over those 15 years. Heck, she'd been in college, then grad school, then she got married and had children! When did she have time to collect hours working horses?

But she was frustrated with her horsemanship because she felt like after "15 years" in horses, she should have been further along than she was. However, when she added up her hours, she found that, actually, she was exactly where she should be in her horsemanship considering how many hours she'd put in. Then, she was able to deal with herself fairly and have realistic expectations for herself and her horse, and she could take pride in maintaining her career, her marriage, her children, AND her horsemanship.

All of us have limitations on how many hours we can collect over time. Many of us have families, jobs, and other commitments. But I'd also propose that we make choices that can either maximize or minimize the hours spent on horse work. There is no substitute for doing the work. No book, no DVD, no daydream can replace the actual hands-on experience of working with horses. All that other study helps, of course, but we still have to go out and do the work. We talk about how the horses are the best teachers, but then I think some of us end up spending more time reading books, watching videos, and talking about horses on Facebook than we do actually putting our hands on them.

We can't expect to skip levels. Sometimes we're in such a hurry to be somewhere else that we don't get everything we can out of the level we currently inhabit. I've done this myself on my own journey. It's kind of like entering a gorgeous valley at a national park and then looking around wondering how soon you can leave to see what's on the other side of the valley walls. When we do that, we can't take in what's in front of us. Maybe it's one of those Zen things that, sometimes, in order to move forward in our horsemanship, we need to be still for a bit and be happy (but not satisfied) with where we are in the present. Maybe that gives us the chance to squeeze every last drop of knowledge and mastery out of that level. I don't know.

There's another wrinkle in this thing about working with horses and putting in the time it takes. I think we need to realize that as we do our work, we do our OWN work. Many of us have a mentor, instructor, or other expert figure who we admire, learn from, and attempt to emulate. We may try to do their work, but only they can do their work. Only Ray Hunt can do Ray's work. Only Buck Brannaman can do Buck's work. No one else can do Buck's work. Buck's work is only Buck's when he's doing it. The same is true for Ray Hunt and Harry Whitney and Pat Parelli and everyone else you can name. Their work is only theirs when they are doing it. Our work is ours. We cannot do someone else's work, and they cannot do ours.

In their work is their feel, and in our work is our feel. I believe that when we touch or make contact with a horse (physically or mentally), whether it's a casual touch or the offer of a cue or a direction, everything we have ever been taught, everything we believe about ourselves, everything we believe about the world around us, every relationship we've ever been in, every horse, dog and human we've buried, every test we've passed or failed, every riding lesson we've taken, every time we've fallen off, every book we've read, every landscape we've admired, all our hopes for the future and our fears of the present are in that touch.

Our touch and someone else's touch, like that of our teacher, though they may look similar or even identical to the horse, are completely different. And this, in large part, is what makes OUR WORK, OUR WORK. We cannot do someone else's work, and, really, we can only imitate someone else's work in the most superficial of ways.

"Do your time," everyone told me. I get that. What they didn't tell me was that no matter how much I studied with "who" or what my "hour count" was, it was always going to be my very own work, and there was no other way. And I had to find a way to be okay with that, because what each of us has to offer the horse is just all of us, everything. That's all they ask for.

Chapter 19

··

Half-Broke Horses

Long ago, when I was on the road full-time helping students with their horses, one of the things I looked forward to was the opportunity to see about 200 horses a year and to start to identify patterns and trends in that population. It felt like I had a very special opportunity to collect and then collate a lot of anecdotal data.

Two patterns became very clear and consistent as I collected my data on the road. The first pattern was that most of my students appeared to be, for the most part, women returning to horses after decades away while they got their careers and/or families going. Some people call these riders "re-riders." These women may have not ridden at all, or maybe they rode a little or (more rarely) a lot as a kid. And there they were, as adults, realizing a lifelong dream to have a horse or horses in their lives. This was the most typical student at my clinics.

The second pattern I saw during those years was the large number of what I would call "half-broke horses" in the general equestrian population and at the clinics. By half-broke horse, what I mean is a horse who has a few, many, or gaping holes in his training, rendering him everything from a little spooky or maybe pushy on the ground to totally unusable and dangerous.

Now, I can hear what you're thinking. These two patterns, put together, are not necessarily a good thing! But it's a pretty easy thing to see if you look around a bit. It's not hard, whatever horse community we're a part of, to find a lovely, well-meaning, ever hopeful beginner/intermediate, often middle-aged rider with a half-broke horse.

I guess I began to see this quite a few years ago, but I didn't quite know what it was. I saw many horses and riders at clinics over the years, and sometimes nothing would get better over the years, and sometimes it would. As I watched and learned and did the work with my students and their horses, what I began to see was that if a horse was half-broke and we did not go all the way back to the beginning of the "hole" (missing information) and install it, the horse didn't change or get better or feel better. Sometimes, I could teach the person to avoid the pitfalls of the hole or holes, but that didn't seem like a good long-term solution. It was like I was helping the student make a map of a field full of land mines rather than helping them remove the land mines for good. I've become a big believer in removing the land mines once we're aware that they're out there. I think we'd all agree that it's just safer that way.

A half-broke horse can look high-spirited, anxious, troubled, difficult, quirky, or obviously poorly trained. A half-broke horse may not tie or understand physical restraint. They may not be comfortable with a rider on their back. They may be scared of being blanketed or saddled. They may not be okay with a flag or ropes other objects or stimuli around them. A lot of times, to recognize a half-broke horse, we have to let go of the horse's age and story and look at him like he's a three-year-old colt. If he were a three-year-old colt, would we ride him? Would we consider him safe and well-educated? Would we say he had a thorough and quality foundation? If the answer to any of those questions is "no," then we probably shouldn't be riding him, no matter his age or story, because we're really rolling the dice on when those holes might turn catastrophic.

So, how do we, as a community, end up with so many half-broke horses? There are any number of ways, but it's pretty easy to skip certain foundation skills in the starting process. Not every horse was started very thoroughly or got a lot of experience in those formative months and years in the beginning. Maybe the horse was started and then turned out for many years, and he went a little "feral" again. Maybe he had a good foundation at one time, but he's been handled with inconsistency and lack of skill since then. All kinds of stuff can happen that leads to a half-broke horse. The why isn't quite as important as recognizing the fact itself. Mostly, a half-broke horse is a half-broke horse.

When I was on the road, there was a clinic I'd been doing for years. One year a new student came, and she had a really good-looking Quarter Horse gelding. I asked her what she needed help with, and she said she needed help getting the horse to go forward consistently. I'd never seen the horse before, and I asked her lots of questions about what she HAD done to work on the problem. We decided that we would work on her timing by starting with a small cue (her "ideal" cue) and then backing it up with a larger secondary cue, which we decided would be the end of her split rein. If, when she cued with her ideal cue, he didn't go, then she'd tap him with the end of her rein. I asked her if she'd tapped him with her rein before, if he would be okay with that, and she said that she had and he would.

So, we began to work on that, and the first time she tapped him with the end of her rein, he bucked her off.

Simply put, she had a half-broke horse. As I continued to help her with the horse over the weekend, we found a whole bunch of things the horse was not okay with. It wasn't hard to dig around and light him up in some way. It felt to me like he was completely confused about a lot of stuff. This rider had been "getting by" right until she wasn't. If he'd been mine, I'd have completely restarted him so that I knew what was in there and what wasn't. That's what I recommended to her, but I don't know what she decided to do.

The better I've gotten to know my students, the higher my standard of what constitutes a "broke" horse has become. Most of my students are not professional-quality horse trainers, nor do they want to be. Most of them are not bronc riders, nor do they want to be. Most of them want to be safe, enjoy their horse time, and learn more as they go along.

It seems to me that the best fix for a half-broke horse is to go back and fill in the holes in order to build, and then maintain, that foundation that got missed or undone somehow. Sometimes, this is simple and easy; other times, it's more complex and challenging. It's always easier to build a foundation before the rest of the building is put on top, but it's possible to put a foundation under an existing building. It's just more complex, and the results won't be quite the same. The same is true of horses. Sometimes, as we work on that foundation, things are going to come apart more and more, kind of like opening Pandora's Box. Sometimes. it gets worse (and sometimes WAY worse) before it gets better. Sometimes, it never gets better because the horse can't let go of the trouble that being half-broke has caused him. Other times, we can give the horse some critical information he's been searching for, and then he's good to go right there and then.

The solution for a half-broke horse, if there is one, is training. If the horse lacks confidence, skill, and information, then that's what he needs. And not just any training, but the training that fills in the gaps and holes. The more a horse knows about how the world works and how he can function in it, the calmer and more confident he's going to be. And I'm not talking about a horse being able to do tricks and busy work. I'm talking about a horse understanding the CONCEPTS that he'll be dealing with in the world around him. He must understand restraint. He must understand how to yield to pressure. He must understand how to turn his decision-making over to people. He must understand how to behave, act, and move around people.

Looking at the half-broke horse in a global context, good training is a horse's first line of defense against becoming an unwanted horse. Even a lame but well-trained horse can find a job taking kids or older or timid riders for a spin. But a lame, poorly trained horse has little chance in today's market.

Making sure our horses are comfortable, confident, and well-trained is something we, as horsemen, have control over.

The knowledge is available and accessible. Creating a well-broke horse is hard work, and it's not for everyone. The work is usually tedious, rarely recognized, and sometimes dangerous. But half-broke horses need help filling in those gaps. If we have a half-broke horse, we can fill in those gaps if we know how, learn how if we don't, or have someone do it for us, but, for the horse's sake, it's got to be done, I think.

Chapter 20

....

The 1%: Managing the Corners

How many times have we heard Ray Hunt's famous question, "What happened before what happened happened?"

I wouldn't try to speak for Ray, but when I hear those words, I usually think about the little things that might precede something bigger or more obvious. For instance, before the cow got around through the gate and into the wrong field, her eyes looked through that gate and her ears pointed through the gate. Only then did her feet carry her THROUGH the gate. Beyond that, she may have done a whole bunch of even smaller stuff that we didn't notice that telegraphed what she was going to do. Somebody who didn't know much about cows might think I was a genius for figuring out what that cow was thinking about because they hadn't yet figured out "what happened before what happened happened" like I had. But if they watched and looked for patterns, they'd eventually see it too.

A lot of this goes on with horses. There is a lot of stuff that is so small that, I'm convinced, most of us can't see it or feel it. This is the stuff that happens before what happens happens. It could be the flick of an ear or a pinch in the skin above the eye. Or, it could be smaller or bigger. Each one of us is in a different place where our awareness in concerned, so some of us are going to see or feel things others maybe can't. As we move along and work on it, our awareness improves (hopefully), and we can see and feel more. Then, our ability to know what happened before what happened happened increases.

So, what's my point here? Well, let's talk about this stuff that happens before what happens happens in a specific context. Let's talk about the power and ability we ALL have to help our horses do better in their work with us...and the power and ability we all have to improve our horse work in a very real way. This is the 1%, or what my friend Jim calls "managing the corners." This is VERY important.

What we are talking about here is managing the QUANTITY of change, basically. To explain this, I'm going to make up some numbers, so bear with me. If you know me and my issues with numbers, you know I won't do too much of this.

Let's say that my horse is working for me in our life together perfectly. That's operating at 100%, or with 100 units of positive operation going on. If things are not really the way I need them to be, then I'm operating at less than 100% or less than 100 units. Let's say my horse is pushy and mouthy and bumps into me and won't get in the trailer. Maybe he's operating at about 75% of what would be super good. We need 25 units of change to be operating at a happy 100%.

In this case, there are a couple ways to get those 25 units of change. You could send him to a trainer for maybe two weeks (because you don't have a lot of money to spend on this) of ground work to get some "manners." The trainer can get 25 units of change quickly, so you can have the change you want in the time they've been given. Depending on what's going on, the trainer might have to use higher levels of pressure to cause a change in a short period of time.

The other way to get a change is to use lower pressure over a longer time period — 1% at a time. If we were to work this way, we'd maybe address every little push that horse did with his head while we were haltering and petting him. We'd shift his weight onto his heels rather than his toes when we were standing in front of him. 1%, 1%, 1%, you get the idea. Pretty soon, we'd have the push out of that horse, same as we would with the first method, but it would likely take a bit longer.

Years ago, I had a student at a clinic in the northwest who, by the time she and her horse got to the arena for their lesson, had a very long laundry list of all the things the horse had already done that had displeased her. We talked this through and picked some things to work on for her lesson, but I encouraged this student to think about what the FIRST thing tended to be that caused friction between her and her horse and to start with that 1% next time. The next day, she arrived for her lesson beaming. "How is it going?" I asked. "I realized I didn't like the way she came out of the stall, so I worked on that first, and she's been great!" That's what the 1% looks like.

I'd propose that just about every horse owner with a good awareness level can do the 1% thing. Plenty of folks might NOT be able to do the 25% all at once thing because they might not have the experience or the skill to do something like that. Or, they just might not want to, and that's fine. A lot of what trainers do is cause large percentages of change quickly because the owner didn't or couldn't manage the 1%.

When we in the horse world complain about trainers and their pressure-filled tactics, one of the things that we need to understand is that they could simply be providing what the consumer is asking for— lots of results quickly (which equates to cheaply). More pressure and less time, or less pressure over a longer time: those are kind of our choices.

Furthermore, I think the ability to be aware of and manage the 1% stuff is one of the things that separates truly great horsemen from the rest. These are the people who catch, halter, and bridle their horses a certain way and with a certain feel, because they are managing that 1% (or 1% + 1% + 1%) through the way they do those activities. They've found that by "managing the corners" on a regular basis, they don't have to deal with things that happen after what happened happened because the first thing never happened, if you get my drift.

If you are reading this because you are a student of horsemanship, then getting a handle on this 1% thing could keep you busy FOREVER. It could cause you to examine and explore awareness and then learn what matters and what doesn't, what's connected to what, and how to influence the things that do matter. This can become a lifelong pursuit. If we get serious about it, we'll study the masters and start to recognize all the ways that they "manage the corners."

All this said, both the 1% idea and the 25+% idea are legitimate ways of going about things. There are times when one horse might be grateful for the clarity and efficiency of asking for a large amount of change quickly. That might scare another horse. And some horses might find the 1% way of looking at things to be like water torture. That method might leave him feeling badly about things longer than necessary. It all depends. There is no right or wrong, just different ways of getting things done.

And, if we bring this back around to the horse himself, he lives in a world where it's taken for granted that the 1% matters. In wild horses, the thing that happened before what happened happened could lead to the demise of the whole band, or to social chaos, or to untold suffering in the group. So horses notice this stuff, and they keep track of it. We can serve our horse best by understanding how this idea functions in HIS world and then using it to help him get along in ours.

Many horse people will feel more comfortable and confident with the idea of getting small changes consistently rather than getting big changes quickly. The horse could maybe go more either way. Like a lot of things in horsemanship, this coin has two sides, and both sides are valid, and are "real". So, maybe, at the end of the day, this thing isn't so much about one way being "right" and another way being "wrong," but more about us being aware of what we're doing, the choices we're making, and how those are influencing our horse. After all, he just kind of wants to know that we know.

Chapter 21

What I Learned From ChiChi

Years ago, I had the honor of working with a little PMU (Pregnant Mare Urine) mare in California named ChiChi. As the story went, ChiChi had come to a horse rescue with a halter on. When her halter fell off, she became untouchable, and when I met her, she hadn't been touched in a couple years. ChiChi trimmed her own feet on the rocks and hard ground of the Sierra foothills and was a healthy and strong lead mare in her pasture.

When the rescue invited me to do a clinic in the spring of 2009, they booked ChiChi in for a slot and asked me to do my best to get a halter on her in the four days I was there. I'm happy to say that I failed in that goal, but what I learned with ChiChi in the process was priceless.

I met ChiChi in a smaller pen that the rescue had set up on a rocky hillside in ChiChi's pasture. ChiChi was standing in the pen, an asymmetrically shaped rectangular-ish pen with a tree in one corner. I saw her as a little (maybe 14.2 hand) homozygous bay tobiano mare with a number tattooed on her left crest and a brand on her left hip. When I climbed into the pen, she tried to climb out. She was clearly frightened of people. It was pure, unadulterated fear, nothing else. "I don't think she wants to be that way," the director of the rescue said. It wasn't long before I agreed with her.

I figured if I was in ChiChi's shoes, I would be scared—REAL-LY scared—but if I was that scared, I thought, I'd want someone to be straight and honest with me. I wouldn't want someone to creep around me and try so hard not to scare me that it had the opposite effect. So, that's what I did. It was tough going for both of us. I made mistakes, and I hit a couple home runs. My first home run was agreeing with her that she could use the fence to support her when I touched her.

What ChiChi was dealing with—that degree of fear and desire to just flee, run far, far away—was really difficult for us humans to imagine. I finished with her for the day and thought about her all night. I didn't know how the heck I was going to get a halter on her.

On day two, ChiChi met me in the middle of the pen and "said" it would be okay for me to touch her out there without the fence for support. I'd brought a string with me that I hoped to get around her neck. I didn't know how or when; that was as much of a plan as I had. I stroked her more that day, and I scared her silly once by getting one of her mane hairs stuck underneath one of my fingernails and tugging on it by accident. But she moved on and went right back to work, and by the end of day two, I was able to move around her with the string and rub her neck, back, and chest.

I didn't get a halter on ChiChi in those four days. I did get a collar on her, from the right side. By the time I moved on, the rescue director and I could enter the pen, fasten an old belt around ChiChi's neck, loop the string through it, and lead her around. The mare looked happy and quiet.

I left California with thoughts of ChiChi running around my head—the feel of her coat, the witch knots in her mane and her quivering fear. I wished and hoped for her to have a good life, one free of fear.

A couple of weeks after I left California, I received an email from the rescue director with a link to a video that she'd taken of herself as she haltered ChiChi out in the pasture, from the left side. Then, she gave her a cookie and took her for a walk.

When I arrived in California to do another clinic at the rescue a year later, I couldn't wait to see ChiChi, but I made myself wait until the clinic was done and my mind was free. I hiked out to her pasture, cookie in hand, and walked right up to her, where I fed her the cookie and stroked her all over. She blinked and sighed, and as I walked around, she followed me. She touched me. It was lovely.

ChiChi didn't "learn something," the rescue director said. ChiChi changed her way of thinking, her beliefs, her life. She decided not to be scared anymore. She decided that people were okay. She just decided. That's sure what it looked like to me.

Why can't we do that? Why is it so hard for us to change? ChiChi decided to change, and she did. That got me thinking pretty hard.

How much does choice factor into what happens to us and what goes on in our lives? Can we make different choices? SHOULD we make different choices? Can we set things up with the horses so they CAN make choices without MAKING them make "our" choices? Are we willing to respect their choices? Is there a way to influence their choices without forcing a sole outcome? Is setting up the choice we want while leaving the "choice" intact the "art" of it all?

Chapter 22

. . . .

If It Walks Like a Duck and Quacks Like a Duck...

It's probably a duck. Be Thorough.

Years ago, when I bought Daisy, a three-year-old Appendix Quarter Horse, I had not yet seen or met her. I bought her based on photos exchanged with the seller via email and the report of a friend who went to see her in person while I was teaching in England. Daisy's breeder/owner told me, truthfully, that she "hadn't done much with her." I did not ask her what she meant by that.

At three years old, Daisy was about 15.3 hands and 1000 pounds when I picked her up. She'd lived on the same farm and with the same horses all her life. Based on her age, her size, her quiet and friendly nature and the fact that the breeder/seller appeared to be an experienced and responsible horse owner, I assumed that she would at least lead, load, tie, and do feet. After all, she'd been handled for three years, right?.

Well, it took about an hour and a half to load her the day I picked her up. Assumption number one was out the window. A couple of days later, it took 20 minutes to lead her out of a 3-acre pasture. Assumption number two gone. So, what did I do? I tied her up and tried to pick up her feet! Assumptions three and four drifted away in the wind.

Thinking back on it now, I'm embarrassed at how many assumptions I made about that filly and how long it took me to fix some of the problems that I created with her due to my assumptions. Leading and loading were the easy ones; it took a good three years for me to get a handle on tying and her feet. Those would've gone a lot smoother for us if I hadn't ignored what my horse was telling me because of the assumptions I'd made that had nothing to do with her.

That was poor horsemanship on my part, plain and simple. If I had simply looked at the horse for what she was at the time, it would have been OBVIOUS where to start with her. But I was blinded by my assumptions, which were based on her age and her size. If it walked like a duck and quacked like a duck, it was a duck. If it acted like a horse who didn't know anything and it looked like a horse who didn't know anything, it probably didn't know anything. It should have been simple.

But lots of us get pretty far from this. We make lots of assumptions about horses based on all kinds of things, like age, breed, size, discipline, good looks or lack thereof, origin, who trained it, or what it's supposedly done previously. We assume a 9-year-old horse that's been ridden is "broke." We assume a big horse is heavy. We assume Quarter Horses are quiet and Arabians are spirited. We assume gaited horses are gaited.

And then there are the ways that expectations color our vision. Your horse doesn't know he wears the mantle of "horse of a lifetime" or "heart horse." He doesn't know he was bred to jump, or cut cows, or run reining patterns. He doesn't know he sold at Keenland as a yearling for $500,000.

In case I needed a reminder of the "Duck" rule, while I was working things out with Daisy, I got a colt in for training who reiterated the lesson. He looked like quite the conundrum when he came in: a foundation-bred four-year-old Quarter Horse gelding with a sweet, quiet, friendly presentation who had some training issues. I found myself wanting to complicate the process of figuring him out, but I decided to take a few weeks to just see what he knew. Very little, it turned out. He didn't lunge or ground drive. He didn't lead great. He had no bend through his body. He was scared of ropes, and he'd hold his breath for saddling. When I told the owner about the colt's concern for ropes, he said he had photos of the horse being roped off of at two and a half years old. I didn't doubt it one bit, but possession of that photo didn't mean that the horse's current owner could rope off him, or even be near a rope on him.

Then, I rode that little horse. I rode him in the round pen, and he felt JUST like a first or second ride colt. Unsteady, unconfident, worried, happy to just stand still and think this through. Then it dawned on me. If it quacks like a duck... This colt FELT like a first or second ride colt, so treat him like one! That was the answer to what I should do with him. If I could do that, we'd get all the holes filled in along the way. Here was this colt who seemed like he should be further along than he was after having been under saddle for two years. But, for whatever reason, he wasn't. Perhaps, if I could meet him right where he was, he could come on through and not have troubles. If he had the tools to understand his job, his world, and the cues he'd be given, maybe he could just feel better.

Since I ran into those two young horses years ago, I've really studied how we get confused about the walking and the quacking and the whole "being a duck" thing. It seems like the human can make this very confusing and can overthink themselves into a tizzy. We all know how "literal" horses are, and that they will behave differently with different people, and if we go far enough down that worm hole, it's just a mess of overthinking.

So, if our horse looks like he's broke, feels like he's broke, and goes like he's broke, he probably is. If he can't calmly lead, tie, catch, load, pick up his feet, saddle, bridle, and/or mount, he probably isn't terribly broke. If we could just see these things with unbiased eyes, everything would be a whole lot simpler.

We owe it to our horses to be thorough. If we leave a hole somewhere now, it's the horse who suffers for it later. When we get in a hurry or let our assumptions blind us, our work becomes about us and not about the horse. If we look and listen and ask questions of him, he'll tell us what we need to know.

Chapter 23

······································

Thoughts on Teaching and Learning Feel

Feel (noun):

1. <u>sensation</u>, feeling

2. the sense of touch

3. *a:* the quality of a thing as imparted through or as if through touch *b:* typical or peculiar quality or atmosphere; *also* : an awareness of such a quality or atmosphere

4. intuitive knowledge or ability

In horsemanship circles, we hear the word "feel" quite often. How does that feel? Take up a feel on the rope/rein. How does the horse feel about that? "...you feel of him, you feel for him, then you both feel together..." (Ray Hunt). Sometimes we use other words— like softness, soft feel, awareness, connection, and life—but we may still be talking about an idea that fits some of the above definitions. No matter the word we choose to represent this concept, we're all talking about the same thing. We may also use the word as a noun, verb, or adjective.

I like definition 3a above, because that one seems very useable. One of the things that the above definitions of "feel" highlight is a range from actually touching to using intuitive (non-touching or "indirect") feel. I think this works for us in horsemanship.

Horses live in a world of feel. You could say that they use a combination of "direct" feel (physical touching) and indirect ("intuitive") feel (non-touching) all day every day. We can see this if we watch horses in a herd interact. They're not terribly verbal, like us. Their communication with each other is based more on visual body language messages and feel/energy. This is why it's important for a horseman to be interested in feel—because it's important to the horses. Our horses are operating based on feel whether we are or not. Thus, we neglect our study of feel at our own peril.

There is a point of view out there in our world that "feel" is something that some people have and others don't. I'm not sure I buy that. Think about children. They have so much feel and awareness. Then, we all grow up, and for various reasons, we lose our feel. We become dull and unaware, and we get rewarded for it. That's what we take to our horses. But in our original, child-like state, we all had a ton of feel and intuition. I choose to believe that we can better our feel through study and hard work. There are a lot of ways to practice improving our feel, from ballroom dancing or meditation to watching and working with horses, which is an essential practice if our goal is to improve our horsemanship.

There's also another view out there that "feel" and "technique" are opposing ideas in horsemanship. I don't think this is so. What I see and experience in my own journey as a horseman and teacher is that feel and technique are essential to each other and tend to improve or harm each other proportionally. They appear to be intrinsically connected, and if we choose, the study of one can lead to further progress in the other. What I see is that if one improves one's feel, then a proportional improvement in technique becomes available. By the same token, if one's technique improves, a comparable improvement in one's feel becomes available. "Available" is the key word there, because folks often don't necessarily capitalize on the improvement available to them in either the area of feel or technique. Do I think feel or technique is more important? Yes.

If we agree that feel is important to horses, that it's an integral part of how they work, then it seems like it would be a good idea for us to work on that in ourselves and with our horses. Many of us have been working with horses for many years with little to no feel or awareness. We can halter a horse mechanically, with no feel, or we can halter a horse with feel and awareness. Both can be done at the same speed (slowing down does not guarantee more feel), both can be done in the same position (high or low, etc.), and both can have the same basic result (a haltered horse). However, if we do things with more feel, we can start to see distant vistas of what might be possible—from having better control for safety to being able to reproduce moments of synergy and connection in movement.

A good place to start working on feel is on the ground. There is a great deal of feel going on with our horses while our feet are still on the ground, and for those of us who are visual learners, we have the added benefit of being able to see AND feel what is going on between us and our horse when we're on the ground. In the round pen, for instance, a drive and a draw have a look to them, but they also have a very distinct feel to them. The horse knows this, and the drive/draw feel and mechanism operate in us and our horse all the time whether we're aware of it or not. In the round pen, with the horse loose, we can practice getting a handle on that feel of drive and draw. Then, we can take that feel into our halter work, our other ground work, and our ridden work. When we work with our horse loose, we are working on our indirect or intuitive feel, and when we put a halter and lead rope on him, we add the element of direct feel through that physical connection. Meanwhile, the indirect or intuitive feel continues simultaneously. Suffice to say that there is a LOT going on with our feel before we ever get in the saddle.

We can learn how to use our reins by learning how to use a lead rope. We can learn how to direct a horse's feet or mind under saddle by feeling our way through that on the ground. If we have no focus on feel until we put a foot in the stirrup, we've just wasted untold opportunities to get a reciprocal feel going between us and the horse. And that's what it's all about in the end: the mystery and the pursuit of feeling the same feels, at the same time, with our horses.

Chapter 24

. . . .

Wherever You Go, There You Are

For quite a few years of my horsemanship journey, I had the privilege of working with almost 200 students every year. Every year, I felt like I was that much further along the path that was my own horsemanship/instructor's journey, and I was often surprised and humbled by the direction that the people and horses I encountered could take me in on my own journey.

I worked for Colorado horseman and clinician Mark Rashid as his full-time assistant for a couple of years, and when I left his employ, I went out on the road myself and picked up quite a few clinics. Thus, those 200 or so students who I got to see every year were from all over the country and some places in Europe too. While all those horses and their people were different in some ways, there were also some "themes" or patterns there. What's interesting is that over the decades that I have spent dedicating my life and work to good horsemanship, the "themes" or patterns in the horse world haven't changed that much.

There were three themes in particular that I noticed back then, on the road, meeting lots of different people and horses. The first of those themes was "holes." For a long time, horsemen I know have spoken of a horse having "a hole" or "holes" in his training.

The term "hole" has been used to mean that a concept or skill has been missed along the way (usually in a horse's formative training) and was found later on (usually due to a problem). Holes are not usually seen as a good thing.

I feel like holes are pretty important to a horse, even if the human is unaware of them. If a horse has holes in his knowledge base, foundation, experiences, or understanding of his life and work, this can cause him to be anxious, pushy, worried, withdrawn, distracted, or even aggressive. Now, just because a horse is any of those things doesn't necessarily mean he HAS holes in his life, but it CAN mean that sometimes. A horse who has holes in his life can be insecure and unconfident.

Now, what about people (horsemen, in particular) with holes in their horse lives, knowledge base, foundation, experience, and understanding? A horseman with holes can be insecure and unconfident. Pair a horse with holes with a horseman with holes (especially corresponding holes), and it can be a recipe for disaster (or a psychiatrist's couch!!!!).

A good foundation of basic knowledge is immeasurably important for a horse. It seems like there are some foundational skills that every horse should have regardless of breed or discipline. That list of foundational skills will only expand depending on the job the horse is expected to do. A good riding or saddle horse will have a long list of foundational skills, all built, carefully and methodically, one upon the other over years.

It's pretty much the same for people in their horse work. There are foundational skills every horseman should know, and then he or she will spend years adding to that knowledge and skill base, depending on their area(s) of interest or study.

Whenever foundation pieces are missing in a horse or in a person, it will eventually show up. If a foundation piece is missing, it's likely that the pieces that should be built upon that foundation are also missing or shaky. If a horse or a person is going to be truly effective and confident in their work, they must have a good foundation.

Then there are the words. That's another theme or pattern. I love words. I love using them and discovering them and agreeing upon them so that we can all communicate. Only once we agree on meanings can we use words to communicate among ourselves. This is just like working with horses. We must first discuss vocabulary and agree on definitions; only then can we put that vocabulary to work to have discussions.

I think I'm constantly using some different words in my work, as I further explore new ideas, philosophies, and techniques. As I more deeply explore an idea, I may rename it with a word that feels right to me. Sometimes I change words because I've adopted a word that a student used for something that seems especially appropriate and accurate. In some cases, I've adopted more "classical" definitions for words, as these definitions have stood the test of time.

I often ask students what they mean by some of the words they use. What do you mean by 'softness'? What behaviors do you see that cause you to say your horse has 'an attitude'? I used to assume that I knew what people meant by the words they used or that I knew what "most" people meant by the words they used. But once I started asking people more questions, I found out pretty quickly that I was mostly wrong when I assumed I knew what people meant by what they said. It also turns out that there is actually a LOT of information (and often some really critical information via stories) stored or hidden in the answer to the question, "What is it that your horse does that makes you say he's _____? Tell me more about that." Wow, is there a lot of good stuff in there.

I enjoy this process quite a lot. Recently, I've begun dissecting the idea and the word "softness" into some more manageable (for me) ideas and feels and words. This has been really fun, and I hope it has led to a new level of clarity in my mind and with my horses. I find that as new layers of awareness add new meaning to old ideas, new words become necessary to express that new layer. It's very satisfying to me to use a word and see the feel and meaning of that word go through a student and their horse.

The third theme that I seem to be revisiting time and time again (due to it showing up in my own work over and over too) is the idea that there needs to be a logical order to things. This may seem silly and obvious to a fault, but it is not.

For instance, in many cases, halter work needs to come before trailer loading or long-lining work. Until we explain to the horse how to follow the halter and feel of the halter rope, his other work in the halter will lack softness and understanding, and in extreme cases, we might not have control at all. That halter work is also a precursor to his work in the bridle. While we can do things out of order if we wish, it is inefficient and often hard on the horse and on us.

Where the rider is concerned, it is important to learn how to ride. This may sound silly, but many of today's horsemen are women returning to horses after quite a few years away. They may not have been riding at a very advanced level when they stopped riding all those years ago, but many of them are buying horses and just going out and trying to ride them in all sorts of situations. Sometimes this works, and sometimes it doesn't. One would think that it might be prudent to take a few lessons and learn to walk, trot, and canter before heading out over the hills on a 200-head group trail ride. We need to learn to ride, to get an independent seat and hands, and to get fit. Then, we can get some magic happening in the saddle. Think of it this way: as long as we're working on staying on, we can't really work on anything else. First, we learn to stay on; then, we work toward learning basic aids. When we've mastered our use of the basic aids, then we can begin the very long process of blending and refining those aids into invisibility. But we cannot refine an aid if we do not understand its basic version. It just doesn't work that way.

Well, let me rephrase that. We COULD do it that way, but that would leave a hole in our knowledge and experience base, which brings us back to my first point.

Working with horses and becoming an accomplished horseman is hard work that is fraught with frustrations and deep personal challenges. Giving ourselves and our horses good foundations is a substantial challenge in and of itself. This part of my own journey—this new and deeper understanding of the value of a good foundation—has given me a more profound appreciation for all my teachers through the years. It has also made me a more conscientious teacher of all things foundational.

Chapter 25

What is "Broke"?

Iwas driving somewhere on the east coast while talking on the phone to a friend who was preparing to load up and head off to Mule Days in Benson, North Carolina. My friend was trying to decide whether to take his older, "broke" horse to Benson or his younger, less "broke" horse. In the end, he decided he better take the older horse because, "Things could get pretty sideways (meaning, he was likely going to get pretty drunk at some point), and a guy could fall off that horse and he plumb won't leave you in the street."

We had a good laugh about that at the time. It kind of stuck with me, though, and I got to thinking about it a bit more, as I sometimes do with stuff like that. Sometimes the profound is hiding in the mundane.

Isn't that what we ALL want, in one way or another? We all want a horse who won't leave us. We'd like him to stay with us physically, of course, and better yet, we'd like him to stay with us mentally.

I got to thinking about what a "broke" horse is. Now, I don't tend to get hung up on that word anymore. That's not to say I like it, but it's the term horsemen usually use to describe a good, solid, experienced, and well-trained horse. Rather than fight about the word, let's just move on and talk about the concept.

I'd guess that what counts as a broke horse is different for different people. Actually, I'm pretty sure about that. "Broke" does mean different things to different people. The important thing is that WE know what broke means for us and our horse.

One year, I was short a clinic horse as I got prepared to head out on the road for the season. My friend, Jim, offered his good horse, Clint for me to use. "Lend me your best horse? Are you sure?"

"I am," said Jim, and he handed me the lead rope to his best horse.

"What do I need to know?" I asked.

"Nothing," Jim said. "Just care for him as if he was yours, and everyone will do great."

That's when I learned that a horse could have a super short "Owner's Manual" and that maybe that could be a good thing. Jim trusted that Clint would adjust to me and I'd adjust to Clint, and he knew that we would figure it out without an "Owner's Manual." That made a huge impression on me. I don't know that I'd ever known a horse before that didn't have a very large "Owner's Manual" full of "dos and don'ts" and "what ifs."

Maybe each of us needs to consider what it is our horse needs to be, to know, and to be able to do to count as broke in our world. If he's not broke, then we need to help him get there to the best of our ability. It could be that he simply doesn't have the mind that we wish he had (but that someone else would think is perfect), or maybe he doesn't have the training or experience that would help him be broke in our world.

Now, one of the things I'm touching on right here is something my friend Jim calls "deciding what the standard is." Jim knows how he'd like a horse to do all the tasks he's being asked to do. That's "the standard." So, Jim might ask me how my new horse loaded, say, and I might answer, "We've got a little ways to go to standard." Or we might look at a quiet, hipshot horse tied to a hitch rail and point out that it seems very "to standard".

As I think about how broke my horses are (or aren't), I'm talking about that standard, really. Here, I will use myself as an example, because I'm not that comfortable speaking for anyone else. Let's talk about the "clinic horse" of my past, for instance. I kind of "collected" horses when I was on the road, and I got to kind of study those horses as I tried them in that job. Being on the road with a horse who wasn't working out was quite a steep learning curve!

So, I'll share what I look for in my broke or potential-to-be-broke clinic horse. This is by no means a cut and dried thing because there are so many variables. It might be okay for a horse to be weak in one area if he's super-strong in another. And I certainly don't worry about something that's superficial or easily changed. What follows is not an exhaustive list of what makes a broke horse in my world, but it's a start and a general framework for the sake of provoking thought and discussion.

I'm going to start with the mind. Sometimes we can get distracted by a horse's resume, history, physical talents or even color. For a clinic horse, I need a horse with a quiet disposition, one who's quiet in the pasture even when no one's looking. My clinic horses need to get along well with other horses and be quiet around food. If a clinic horse can share food, that makes him even better as a traveling clinic horse. If his predisposition is to think and figure things out rather than panic when stuff is happening around a horse clinic, he is much more suited to the lifestyle.

My broke horse is good on the ground. He ties, anywhere, any time. He's quiet when he's tied. He doesn't chew on anything or paw or get impatient. He doesn't tear up my stuff. He leads softly, gives me my space, and can yield when asked. He doesn't run people over or bang into them. He catches and halters anywhere, any time. For me, my broke horse accepts a blanket loose in the field.

More than anything, my broke horse doesn't hurt anyone—in particular, my equine health care professionals like the vet, chiropractor, and/or farrier. This, for me, is non-negotiable.

My broke horse loads—anywhere, any time—without a struggle. He's quiet in the trailer and only comes out when he gets the cue.

Then there's riding. My broke horse saddles, bridles, and mounts quietly. He goes, stops, turns left, turns right, and backs up as softly and nicely as he can for the level he's presently at. The "standard" for this work will change as the horse advances in his age and training.

Depending on what "extra" job my horse is going to do, there'll be some other stuff that he needs to know or to gain some degree of mastery in. For example, horses who pony other horses need to be relatively "flat" (emotionally unresponsive) to the other horse while doing that job. That's not the time for herd dynamics. Horses who jump need to be careful with their legs and soft in the bridle in front of and after the jumps. Foxhunting horses need to be terribly kind to hounds no matter what the hounds do. Cow horses need to be comfortable and confident around cows and timely in accepting direction.

At the end of the day, my broke horse seems to exude a patient, "what can I do for you today?" attitude, and he has the skills, training and experience to deliver more times than not.

Your description of what a broke horse is in your world might be very different than mine. A working cowboy is going to have a different description of a broke horse, as will a Grand Prix dressage rider. Neither description is "wrong" or "right"; they're just different perspectives, that's all. Different perspectives from different worlds; all are valid to those who hold them.

Like most all things in horsemanship, I think that we need to know what we're looking for. If we don't have a clear picture of what we're looking for, it can lead to frustration, disappointment, and general unhappiness for everyone involved. I don't know that it's fair to the horse to not know what we want/need and how we're going to help him get there or not (as the case may be).

In the end, I think what we all want is a horse who won't leave us, who can stay with us, who WANTS to be with us. That doesn't just happen. It seems to come from a slightly mysterious combination of natural predisposition, training, and experience. That goes for the person AND the horse.

So, what is broke in your world?

Chapter 26

On Judging Progress

I just picked up a new project horse. After two and a half years, my last project horse has ascended to the #1 saddle horse position, so I've been thinking a lot about fair and reasonable ways to judge progress in both horses and people.

Like a lot of things in horsemanship and in life, we seem to get ourselves stuck in the extremes; either we judge too harshly or too sympathetically and, thus, judge equally unfairly. It is harmful for people AND for horses to either be given an A for D-quality work or to be given a D for A-quality work. Depending on our personality, we might have a predilection toward one or the other of those things, and I think that's a good thing to know about ourselves.

Many of us have been attracted to so-called "natural horsemanship" because we are looking for a softer and quieter way to get things done with horses. In some cases, that desire for softness and quietness and relationship has caused us to err on the side of caution (we don't want to be harsh) so perhaps we've given horses and people As for D-quality work. This is just as injurious as the opposite. I'd propose that giving high grades for low-quality work is a good way to kill off the try in the student.

Why try harder or offer more if the current level of effort is getting me to the top of the class? However, if I can get a fair grade, then I can figure out if I need to try harder or not. I can sleep in the bed I've made, so to speak, and that would make sense to me if it was consistent.

I think I'm looking for "authenticity" in horsemanship, including clarity and fairness and understanding on both sides. That may be soft and gentle sometimes, and not so much other times. Sometimes my horse and I may ask each other to try harder. Sometimes, we'll give each other high grades; other times, we'll give each other lower grades. That feels authentic to me.

And then there's the idea of time frames. I've been thinking about the fairness of asking horses and people to make monumental changes in a clinic in just a few days —a few hours, actually. Because of the format we work in, we're judging our horses and our riders on a daily basis, and we see often some miraculous things happen in just a few days. However, we also hear about how the "clinic glow" wears off and things go back to the way they were when it's just the horse and the person again. So how deep did that change that took just a few days to accomplish go?

It makes more sense, sometimes, to judge on a longer-term basis. At home, we may judge a training horse by the month, because the owner is paying by the month. We may judge our own professional saddle horses annually. No one at the farm, horse or human, is judged by the day, really. But at a clinic, we're judging by the day. What affect does that have on our work and our perspective of ourselves and our horses?

It's all about balance. Both extremes exist and are true, and both extremes (long-term and short-term judgement) are valid in different situations. Baby behavior, for instance, can be cleared up quickly—sometimes in moments, but often in days or weeks— so if we've been seeking a change for years, something's likely not going the right way. If what we're looking for is a higher level of finesse in our broke horse, that's going to take long periods of time. Working with a troubled or remedial horse is going to take long periods of time. The extremes and everything in the middle are all fair when applied appropriately. So, there are some things that are realistic to see change in a clinic situation, while there are other things may take years of clinics to see cumulative progress.

My theoretical new project horse is not going to get an at-home four-day clinic and be expected to be good to go. Whoever this horse is, he or she needs a fantastic foundation, and I might as well plan on many days of what feels like "going to the office": leading, halter work, trailer loading, tying, picking and holding up feet, accepting ambient energy, field trips away from home, manners at feeding time, hobbling, rope work, flag work, round pen work, inside turns, outside turns, drive and draw, lunging, etc. I could go on and on. That's just a start. This is going to take months, and the horse is going to have their own part in how fast or slow it goes.

I think we get in the (bad) habit of judging daily, and, truth be told, there are probably pretty few situations where it's actually necessary or fair. Earlier in my horsemanship journey, I came home every day defeated, in tears, frustrated to no end, because I was judging me and my horse daily, and we were, honestly, trying to do a new, hard thing well. That was not a fair way to judge either of us.

This daily judging method leads to a very emotional, up-and-down kind of experience in our horsemanship. It also puts a lot of pressure on our horses (and ourselves), because if we do this, a "bad" session with our horse will likely ruin our day.

What's the "trend" in our work? Are we slowly, steadily trending forward? Are we trending forward in fits and starts (more common than smooth trends), with maddening plateaus and occasional hiccups backward? Are we checking off more boxes of things we want to do with our horse, or are we unchecking boxes, over time? Do we need to keep a diary to track this progress so that we can look back in six months or a year and judge for SURE whether we're going forward or backward?

I don't know if I could tell you when the last time was that I had a "bad" session or ride with any of my horses. I just don't keep track of it like that anymore. I'm tracking where we are, what we can and can't do, and I'm comparing that with my goals or necessities. But I view it in a very neutral way now. This, in turn, allows me to stay much more emotionally neutral and, therefore, more consistently available for my horses.

Chapter 27

· ·

Filling In

"**F**illing in" is a term I heard a long time ago in the horse-manship culture. I might have read about it in the old *Trail Less Traveled* magazine (the predecessor to today's *Eclectic Horseman* magazine), and it obviously made an impression on me because, although I don't hear it much anymore, it has stuck with me for well over 20 years.

"Filling in," in general terms, refers to the horse's ability to do something right even though the human somehow messed up the cue, presentation, or request or just plain got in the way. A horse fills in when he does something correctly even though we asked incorrectly or inaccurately. Filling in does NOT refer to a horse who is "programmed," over-schooled, frightened, or bullied into rote behaviors. In my mind and experience, true filling in is an act of understanding and generosity on the part of the horse.

There seem to be two factions at the extremes in the horse world today: the people who think that everything a horse does is "right" and anything he does "wrong" was caused by the human present, and those who think that everything the horse does "wrong" has nothing to do with the human present and is purely the horse's "fault." Neither of these models forms a framework for a working partnership based on give-and-take and mutual respect and trust. It might be possible to be somewhere in the middle. Sometimes I will make a change, and sometimes I'll ask my horse to make a change. No one is to "blame," but both parties have responsibilities within the relationship. That may not be what you're looking for with your horse and that's fine, but it is what I think I am striving for.

So, let's look at filling in and why it might be a good thing. If a horse can fill in (do the right thing when the human does the wrong thing), they can likely be handled and ridden by a variety of people. The horse who can fill in will make pretty accurate guesses when cues that look or feel a little different come across. Filling in could make a horse pretty useful in some circles. For instance, filling in is an essential skill for a school horse or child's horse. New riders and children often do not have the ability to combine accurate visualization, focus, and cues consistently; therefore, they depend desperately on a horse's ability to fill in. The first time a beginner rider accidentally loses their balance and grabs on with their legs to steady themselves, the horse needs to fill in and know that's not a canter cue!!!! None of us could have learned to ride without the help of a bunch of horses who could fill in. Where I came from, we called them saints, talked about their halos, and generally worshipped the ground they walked on. In the riding schools I rode in and grew up in, these horses were revered and highly respected.

Filling in is also an essential skill in any horse we may sell or move in some way to a new home (that would include "rescue" horses). In order to succeed in a new home, a horse is going to need to be able to fill in and try to do things correctly even though the human's presentation may be different than what they're used to or lacking in some way. Ideally, the horse will only need to fill in for a period of time, until the horse and their new owner begin to occupy some common ground together.

Another, more sophisticated level of filling in is about the horse understanding CONCEPTS rather than CUES. I think a horse has a better chance of being able to fill in if he understands concepts rather than just responding to cues accurately. This discussion can get us into some pretty urbane areas that I'll save for another time, but suffice to say, helping a horse understand how to fill in isn't about dumbing him down or dulling him out. Teaching concepts is about feel and timing and balance. Teaching concepts is about teaching a horse to learn and to think on his feet, in the moment. This is good stuff.

So, what would filling in look like? Well, take me, for instance. I have a neurological deficit on my left side that causes me to ride asymmetrically most of the time, but my horses can travel straight and take both leads. Why? Because they fill in for me. I do it as correctly as I can for them, and then I ask them to pick up the leftover slack, so to speak. It makes for a pretty cool partnership, because I recognize their generosity in filling in for me.

Years ago at a clinic, I got a bad cold and ran a pretty good fever for a day. I knew I had just enough energy for my students but not much for my horse that day. When I got my horse out that morning, I knew I had very little to offer him, but I trusted that he had a lot to offer me that day. He offered me a comfortable place to sit and energy to draw off of, and I never heard a peep of complaint from him. That felt like partnership to me. I thanked him for his generosity and cleverness and felt much better the next day, partly due to the fact that he took no energy from me the day before.

Years later, I had a pretty scary fall with a horse that left me concussed and with broken ribs. I was a bit spooked, to be honest, because I really thought my judgment was better than that. It really dinged my confidence in my ability to read a situation. When I was healed up enough to ride my good saddle horse, I just kind of "told" him, "Hey, buddy. I'm going to feel pretty weird for a little while. It's not about you, okay? I don't doubt YOU. I doubt myself right now, but I know you can help me trust myself again." And he did. There were times where I was overtaken by waves of anxiety, or I'd freeze up, and that horse just took care of things. He was a good partner during that time.

When I was training horses for the public, it was essential that I understood filling in, or I would have produced horses that the owners couldn't ride or work with. In that scenario, it may be safest to produce a horse who's looking to meet the human in the middle and who has a certain tolerance for variation in the human's presentation. This is something we can prepare him for if we're thinking about it.

Any working horse will need to be able to fill in. As a rider, once we start doing a "job" on horseback, part of our awareness, mind and body will go to that job and will leave the horse in a place where he may well need to fill in for us. Folks who do real jobs with horses prize horses who can fill in and nearly do the jobs themselves.

There are certain horses who may never be able to fill in for a human. Those are mostly troubled or scared horses, horses who are in need of lots of filling in from the human. These horses can be a great lesson in how a human can fill in for a horse, but they may offer us little opportunity to explore the reverse. Due to their inability to fill in, these horses are often inappropriate for beginners and can suffer greatly when they have to be handled by lots of different people.

So, let's say you've decided that you'd like your horse to fill in for you some and maybe be able to fill in for some other people. What should you do? This doesn't have to be very complicated at its simplest level. Helping a horse figure out how to fill in can be as easy as sometimes asking him to complete a task correctly even though you may have communicated inaccurately or gotten in his way. Doing this with awareness and mindfulness is not the same as doing it out of ignorance, though one could argue that the result of both can be pretty similar (a generous, understanding horse who can fill in). I'd also do things like prepare horses for people who will pet (slap) them rudely and touch them in not-so-friendly places. If we just think about some of the things our horse might run into in his world, we'll see all kinds of places where he could fill in for the human.

True filling in is a window into the horse's generosity of spirit. My own awareness of when my horses have filled in for me has given me some of my most sublime moments with my horses. And, although I may be dreaming it, I think that knowing how to fill in for me helps them to appreciate my efforts all the more when I try very hard to get everything really right but fail.

"It's amazing what a horse will get done in spite of them, and if he didn't fill in, we wouldn't get much done with horses. It's amazing what the horse will do for us if we treat him like he's one of us." - Ray Hunt

Chapter 28

How I Almost Quit

I almost quit in 2014. For real. I was ready to throw in the towel, sell all the horses, clear the place out, cancel all my work, take down the website, and get a job in town. I was done. Finished. I was too tired, frustrated, and heartbroken to go on another minute. I could no longer carry on living with the misery in my horse life.

I am sharing this story with you because it is part of who I am and how I work now, and I know that some of you out there may someday end up in the same spot I was in, and maybe knowing how someone else got through it will help you in that moment. I hope so. I don't want any of us to quit.

When I married Glenn in January 2013, he asked me what I WANTED to do with horses. Not what I HAD to do, but what I WANTED to do. For the first time in my life, I had my own farm, was my own boss, and could design my own horse program from the ground up. What did I want that to look like? Boy, I didn't know! I'd been scrambling to live paycheck-to-paycheck for so long that I wasn't quite sure how to actually CHOOSE something for any reason other than an economic one. But I gave it some thought, and I decided that I would follow my life-long dream of rehabilitating Thoroughbred racehorses and reselling them as riding horses. Meanwhile, I'd keep doing clinics and blend my horsemanship and foundation work into the Thoroughbred business at home.

Our first TB arrived at the farm in February of 2013, an uncut three-year old colt with a knee chip. Adding more and more of them was easy – heck, you can get them for free!!!!!! We turned two stalls in our barn into "hospital stalls" and built some small turnout pens. I found a great babysitter horse to turn out with the stallions until they were gelded, and with a mix of rehabs and restarts, I was very soon developing six TBs.

Needless to say, I started hemorrhaging money. My vet was by at least once a week. A lot of the horses could rehab barefoot, but some of them, even if not in work, were so wonky that they needed shoes just to be comfortable in the field. Most of them were hard-keepers, and my feed bill skyrocketed. There were only a couple I could put under saddle right away because of the down-time they needed off the track. Very quickly, I was doctoring, cleaning stalls, feeding, feeding again, running off my feet with bug sheets, turning fans on and off, and not riding at all. It may have been my dream, but it wasn't quite turning out like the Cinderella stories I read on the Facebook OTTB groups.

Many of the physical rehab horses healed well only to develop other injuries or different forms of unsoundness. One horse turned out to be a terrible headshaker. By the fall of 2013, I was seriously in debt, and I did not have a single horse who could make a dent in paying that debt off. In my whole collection, there was not one horse who was going to sell as a $15,000 hunter/jumper horse, but there was one horse that I'd fallen in love with and wanted to keep: Memphis. So, I held onto that hope as the purpose for the whole exercise...

Memphis came to us in the late spring of 2013. I'd found him through Facebook, and he cost $2500. He was a five-year-old stallion who'd raced 12 times in the year or so before we got him, meaning, according to his records, he hadn't raced until he was four. He was a gorgeous horse: 16 hands and dapple grey. We had him shipped from West Virginia and went to work.

Glenn pulled his shoes (racing plates), and I booked a castration for him. He was a gentleman. He was lovely to handle on the ground, and though he had a scar on a hind leg, he appeared sound. He didn't have the body soreness or obvious types of limb lameness that we'd seen in a bunch of the others off the track, so we were thrilled.

We had him gelded and the next day, turned him out with our gelding herd, where he was instantly accepted. We gave him a few months off, with lots of freedom, forage, and friends, and he thrived. He looked great, was easy to handle, and was just gorgeous, inside and out. "This is THE ONE," I started to think. THE ONE.

In fall of 2013, I began to start Memphis on some ground work. He was so thoughtful and had so much try. Though what I was asking of him was different from what he knew, he went with me. He said "yes" a lot. He adapted well to the western saddle, and I put some rides on him in the round pen.

In my mind, everything about him was perfect. Not too big, not too small, enough body to take up my leg, no baggage, an amazing mind, a willingness to try anything. Before long, I was throwing a rope off him, helping him find his right lead, and riding him out in the fields by himself.

Then, one day, he didn't come in for dinner. That's never good, as horse people know. I grabbed a halter and went to find him out in the pasture. There he was, standing in a corner of the field, bearing no weight on his right front, his fetlock as big as a cantaloupe.

He hobbled and hopped to the barn, ever kind and accommodating. I put in a frantic call to the vet. He said to cold hose it and wrap it and he'd be out first thing in the morning. So, that's what we did. Memphis continued to not bear any weight on the leg.

We did x-rays the next day, and though the images were slightly "inconclusive," our vet was concerned about a possible fracture and recommended a trip to the university hospital, where they had better diagnostic tools.

So, we made an appointment for him and, in the meantime, treated him like a precious egg, with deep shavings, lots of hay nets, and friends outside his stall door. We filled the trailer with shavings and carefully drove him the two hours to Auburn for diagnostics. The vets at Auburn were able to rule out a fracture, but then we had a different problem: if it's not a fracture, what IS it? Why is he so lame, and why is there so much swelling?

Auburn sent him home with anti-inflammatories, and we planned to take him back for more diagnostics after the swelling had come down some more, when they could get better images.

Back to Auburn again, and ultrasound imaging showed some "dirty" joint spaces in his front fetlocks. In other words, it looked like there might be some stuff in there that didn't belong there. The vet recommended exploratory arthroscopic surgery to insert a camera into his joint spaces in his front fetlocks to get a clearer picture of what was going on. Depending on what they found, then, they could also clean the joints up arthroscopically as well.

My vet bills on Memphis, once we added this procedure, were nearing $5000. I didn't know where the money was going to come from, but I consented to the surgery. I just wanted Memphis to be well again.

It was a couple of days between when we dropped Memphis off and when they did the surgery. Glenn was out of town on a business trip the day of the surgery, so I was at the farm alone, working with our other OTTBs and waiting for the phone to ring.

The phone rang, I picked it up, and the vet said that Memphis was out of surgery and recovering well. Whew. Great! Findings? Well, what they'd found was that Memphis basically didn't have any cartilage left in either of his front fetlock joints. I proceeded to ask the vet about what kind of life Memphis could have, and she said that by the age of 10, he would be likely unrideable and that a "very light riding" career might be possible until then, with medical maintenance.

I remember what I said: "Put him down. Why didn't you call me while he was on the table?"

The vet was shocked, I think. They have a rule that when you want to end a horse's life at the hospital and you're not there, you have to say it on the phone to two vets. I did that. Then, I hung up the phone and sat in a corner of the tack room and cried for a very, very long time, until way after dark.

I was crushed. The one horse I had banked on was dead. The others were virtually worthless. I was buried in debt. There was nowhere to borrow any more money. I had made too many mistakes, and I was completely spent emotionally and physically. I began to have anxiety attacks at night, where I'd wake up feeling like there was a metal band around my chest and I couldn't breathe. I had nightmares that the horses had broken out and were running on the road. I imagined I had left barn doors open and gates unchained. I was going crazy.

I saw my local doctor, and he put me on anti-anxiety medication and muscle relaxers and recommended that I see a mental health care professional to learn how to master my anxiety. It was not a good time in my life.

I decided to quit. I started giving away and selling my remaining Thoroughbreds for cheap just to get the anxiety off the farm. With no horses, I didn't have to picture them running down the road. I looked forward to a job in town – the 9 to 5 hours, heat and a/c, a steady paycheck, nice clothes. Respect. Appreciation. Rewards. I was done. I could ride Glenn's horses when I got the urge, and that would be fine. I went to see the counselor.

I didn't quit, as you know. I followed the advice of the counselor, and I took control of my anxiety and my thoughts. Then, I took control of my environment.

I made a lot of mistakes when I tried to follow my dream of rehabbing OTTBs. I know there are a lot of people who are really good at that job, but I'm clearly not one of them. Having a dream and a lot of passion were not enough. I had hoped they were, but that wasn't the case for me. My dream broke me, and standing here with the benefit of hindsight, I'm glad of it. I'm glad because when I broke, I had to reconsider, reconstruct, and reinvent in a more conscious and deliberate way than I ever had before. I had to take responsibility for my own misery and unhappiness. I learned that I had made an environment for myself that made me miserable, and I ran the risk of walking away from ALL the horses in the world because of my experience with a FEW horses. I let that experience kill my passion. That was a choice.

When Memphis died, my dream quite literally died with him. I think that at that point I had to get all the way back to my "why" ~ my original why, not the "current" why. I had to get back to why I ever took that first riding lesson, because I am still that same person. At the end of the day, my "why" remained. It survived. My why? Because horses are beautiful and fascinating, and I can't stop thinking about them. Because that's how I am made. It's not so much that I'm tough, or stubborn, or driven, or have any of those admirable character traits. It's simply that I'm a girl who is fascinated by horses and not interested in much else. And that why will carry me forward, wherever that is.

I have loved preparing this book for you, and I really hope you have enjoyed reading it.

I realize that there are a lot of ideas presented here, and that ideas need to be converted to actions in order for you to be able to help your horse.

Are you eager to learn how to turn your aha moments into an ever deeper bond with your horse?

I have several learning possibilities for you.

If you want to...

- ❖ Discover ways that horses and humans can pay attention to each other

- ❖ Empower your horse to tackle the human world with confidence and thoughtfulness

- ❖ Become the kind of person your horse enjoys spending time with

- ❖ Learn to create the physical and mental balance that leads to refinement on the ground and under saddle

To find just the right learning option for you, visit http://www.ethosequine.com/courses

See you over there.

Kathleen

Made in the USA
Middletown, DE
19 September 2023

38769432R00073